Automak

In

ı to

ent

John W. Capobianco

Automate Your Network
by John W. Capobianco
Cover photo taken at the San Diego Zoo by John W. Capobianco
Copywrite © 2019 John W. Capobianco. All rights reserved.
Date: March 2019

I dedicate this book to my wife. You have always loved me, supported me, and encouraged my mad dream of becoming a real IT professional and now an author. Without you I would never have found the courage to write this book. I love you.

Table of Contents

Preface

Thank you and welcome to "Automate Your Network".

Today's modern networks have grown in scale and complexity while the tools and methodologies used in designing, operating, and deploying these networks have largely remained stagnant. Network automation begins with automating network reconnaissance. This is accomplished by gathering important information from network devices while building a library of dynamic on-demand utilities and generating living documentation. The next step is making automated changes to the network. Starting small, the book exhibits the simplicity and elegance of network automation. Next, the book outlines how to automate larger changes that require a high number of repetitive steps. These changes will be executed serially in a specific orchestrated order, making them perfect for an automated solution. After gaining comfort with the new tools, readers can fully transform network configuration management to an automated, intent-based, self-documenting system. Change management and version controls are built into the processes. Once coverage of the network is achieved, a data model driven, dynamic template-based, human-readable version of the network exists. The final step is migrating to a continuous integration / continuous delivery (CI/CD) pipeline, thereby fully automating the network.

Network automation is not a substitute for solid network design or foundational knowledge about networking. Knowing how to convert network configurations to code is not the same as understanding the configurations themselves. It is strongly encouraged that network administrators who understand the configurations be involved in the code conversion processes. Network administrators need to understand the Open Systems Interconnect (OSI) model, achieve industry certifications, and stay current on industry trends while developing their coding skills. Before going too far, here is a basic outline of the book.

How This Book is Organized

This book is divided into two parts: Part 1 introduces network automation while Part 2 contains instructions to begin coding. Part 1 covers what network automation means; why organizations should automate; how to automate; and where to start when ready to automate. Part 2 contains the technical steps, with examples, that can be used as a foundation for network automation.

Part I.

Chapter 1 What Is Network Automation?

Compares traditional network management using a manual approach to network changes and maintaining documentation with modern network automation capabilities. This chapter introduces software-defined networking and the concept of converting networks to code.

Chapter 2 Why Automate the Network?

This chapter covers the problems with traditional network management and how network automation solves these problems. As networks scale in size and complexity the traditional ways of managing them has become inadequate. The tools have finally arrived which allows for the quick delivery of automated solutions with more precision and quality.

Chapter 3 How to Automate the Network?

The modern network management toolkit is described here. The tools required to automate the network include:

- Microsoft Visual Studio Code (VS Code) (*https://code.visualstudio.com/*).
- Microsoft Team Foundation Server (TFS) (*https://visualstudio.microsoft.com/tfs/*).
- Git (*https://git-scm.com/*).
- Linux (Ubuntu (*https://www.ubuntu.com/*)).
- Ansible (*https://www.ansible.com/*).

Chapter 4 Where to Start with Network Automation?

This chapter includes guidelines for launching the automation initiative. Begin with gathering information about the network's current state and gradually start making small tactical changes while building towards larger orchestrated solutions.

Part II.

Chapter 5 Repository Structure

This chapter includes a recommended approach for the repository structure. The skeletal folder structure that holds variables, tasks, templates, Ansible playbooks, and automated documentation that scales with growth.

Chapter 6 Network Reconnaissance

Begin network automation by first discovering and documenting the network. This chapter provides examples of network reconnaissance playbooks that can be used to gather detailed information from network devices.

Chapter 7 Tactical Playbooks

This chapter provides examples of tactical one-time change playbooks leveraging the Ansible **ios_command** module for Cisco devices.

Chapter 8 Data Models and Dynamic Templates

This chapter explains how to abstract data from configurations and create models in YAML (*http://yaml.org/*) and dynamic templates using Jinja2 (*http://jinja.pocoo.org/docs/2.10/*).

Chapter 9 Dynamic Intent-Based Documentation

Utilizing data models this chapter introduces intent-based documentation. The Ansible **assemble** module is introduced along with the Markdown (*https://daringfireball.net/projects/markdown/*) file format.

Chapter 10 Configuration Management

Full automation of network configuration management is achieved in this chapter utilizing the data models and dynamic templates. Complete coverage of the enterprise network is established.

Chapter 11 Continuous Integration / Continuous Delivery

This chapter introduces the CI/CD pipeline. Automated builds and releases for complete network automation using TFS are introduced.

Summary

Appendix A Online Resources

Links to relevant information on the Internet including the "Automate Your Network" GitHub repository accompanying the book. More examples of Ansible data models, templates, and playbooks can be found here.

Who Should Read This Book?

Chief Information Officers / Chief Technology Officers

Technical leaders should read this book to raise awareness of these new modern methodologies for automating an enterprise network. If the organization is currently operating the network using either mostly manual efforts or expensive Network Management Solutions (NMS) consider network automation using the tools and technologies presented in this book. The leaders and influencers in technology can mandate that network operations evolve. Drastic improvements in network downtime, stronger security, adherence to corporate standards and best practices can be realized with automation along with a lean and cost-effective network operation.

Senior IT Directors / Strategists

The impact network automation has on an organization should not be underestimated. With automation comes an entirely new toolkit the organization needs to support and adopt. There are many things senior management need to consider beyond the code itself such as adjustments to current approval processes for change management. Network engineers or administrators need to learn how to convert the network to code. Network operators who currently use the Command-Line Interface (CLI) for changes need to adopt new skills and be able to execute Ansible playbooks. Linux may be new or unfamiliar to the organization and so a comprehensive strategy is essential to the success of any initiatives brought forth to automate the network.

Network Engineers / Designers

Networks still need to be designed. The need for CCIE skills is not replaced by automation, however engineers will adopt new skills and start looking at networks differently by treating them like any other application in the organization. Developing structured data models and dynamic templating logic for scale and quality is the new mission. This transition may come easier to some than others. Programming basics such as writing comparative "if" statements and iterative "for" loops, as well as being able to abstract information from configurations, become necessary skills.

Some engineers will be familiar with the basic programming concepts however there is a natural transitionary period as new tools and technologies are introduced and adopted.

Seasoned Network Administrators

The need for CCNP / CCDP level of knowledge and capabilities is not replaced by automation. In fact, the two go together very nicely. An understanding of IP addressing, routing and spanning-tree is required, as well as knowing how to operate and configure network devices. These skills only enhance the ability to automate a network.

New Network Administrators

Understanding the basics of networking will always be the foundation of a career in IT. However, if new network administrators can learn automation skills in conjunction with learning the fundamentals of networking, it becomes their native way of operating the network. It is a great time to begin with networks and see them as something that can be operated like an application and not just a collection of hardware devices. Novice network administrators may benefit most from network automation because entering the industry during the inception of automation means they develop from the ground up. Careers will grow along with network automation and will no longer suffer the dark ages of manual CLI network management.

Software Developers

The skills of a software developer directly translate to network administration and operations. A basic understanding of networking is required; however software development skills are otherwise directly transferrable. As the network is converted to code there are opportunities for a larger team to contribute to operations with a NetDevOps approach. Software developers can bring ideas and concepts of development to the network team. They can offer to setup a collaboration between developers and network administrators in the organization and convert the network to code together.

Tools Used in This Books

Microsoft Visual Studio Code

https://code.visualstudio.com/

Visual Studio Code (VS Code) is more than just an enhanced text editor, it is a full development environment. Git integrates with VS Code which acts as a Graphical User Interface (GUI) front-end, transforming commands to point and click operations. All the code in this book has been created using VS Code.

This free tool is used by software developers everywhere and can be adopted by network administrators. The base editor will be enhanced by installing extensions used to help write effective, error-free Python code, YAML files, and Jinja templates.

Microsoft Team Foundation Server

https://visualstudio.microsoft.com/tfs/

Microsoft Team Foundation Server (TFS) is a modern source code management system with a built-in reporting engine. Traditionally, TFS has been used for software development and storing application code. From this code software can be built, tested, and released. This book demonstrates how network administrators and operators can now leverage the power of TFS. Moving forward TFS will be the source code repository and is a key part of the branching strategy. Moving all the network configurations into TFS immediately brings the value of source and version control.

Some key features of TFS include:

- The ability to track changes to code.
- Easily identify when and what configurations changed and by which developer.
- The ability to create new branches to isolate changes in development from live production configurations / code.
- The CI/CD delivery pipeline.

Git

https://git-scm.com/

Git is a distributed version control system. Git is very lightweight, portable, and integrates with TFS. Git is referenced often in this book and is a key foundational element of automating a network. Git is very easy to learn yet extremely powerful. By using Git, version control over the network configurations becomes a reality. Git commit history makes it easy to understand exactly what changed, under what branch, and by which developer. Configurations can also be rolled back to a previous point-in-time.

Linux

https://www.linux.org/

Any flavor of Linux can be used to run Ansible. This book focuses on Ubuntu, however Ansible support is not limited to this version of Linux. Fully supported releases of Red Hat Enterprise Linux and Red Hat Ansible Engine are available for enterprises. Ansible will be installed on this Linux system and needs to be able to Secure Shell (SSH) to the network devices being automated. Keep this in mind when placing the Linux system onto the network.

Ansible

https://www.ansible.com/

Ansible is an open source automation framework that provides agentless connectivity agnostically throughout the enterprise. The focus of this book is the network automation capabilities of Ansible. Windows or Linux server administrators, load-balancer or firewall administrators, and application developers can all use Ansible. Ansible has many more capabilities that exceed the scope of this book. "Automate Your Network" primarily focuses on the Cisco IOS modules used to interface with Cisco Catalyst switches.

One thing worth noting is that Ansible is **not** a programming language but rather a framework of tools written in Python; not Java or C++ for the network.

Network Modules

https://docs.ansible.com/ansible/latest/modules/list_of_network_modules.html/

Key components of the Ansible framework are network modules provided by, and developed in collaboration with, hardware vendors like Cisco or F5. This book specifically focuses on the Cisco IOS facts, commands and configuration modules. Be aware that many more modules exist beyond the network modules from Cisco. The same principals outlined in this book for campus enterprise network automation can be applied to other platforms such as a Cisco-based data center, for example, where the Cisco NX-OS modules are available for Ansible.

YAML

http://yaml.org/

(YAML) Ain't Markup Language is a human-readable data serialization standard for all programming languages. YAML is used extensively throughout this book primarily to write data models for Ansible **group_vars** and **host_vars**, Ansible tasks, and Ansible playbooks. Using YAML data can be abstracted from the configurations and can create standard models by platform and function for the network.

Jinja2

http://jinja.pocoo.org/docs/2.10/

Jinja2 is a dynamic templating language for Python used to create templates. These templates are a mix of static text representing Cisco IOS commands, programmatic logic, and dynamic variables. At run time these templates are compiled using the variables held in the **group_vars** and **host_vars** files.

Online Resources

Throughout this book hyperlinks are used to connect the reader to relevant online resources. A GitHub repository has been setup in support of this book as well as an appendix explaining how to use the GitHub repository to clone a copy of the repository locally.

Preface | 7

Part I

"Any sufficiently advanced technology is indistinguishable from magic."
- Arthur C. Clarke

Part I of this book is designed as an introduction to network automation. Chapter 1 defines network automation and compares it to the traditional, manual, network operational model. Chapter 2 explores why organizations should consider network automation. How to automate the network is covered in Chapter 3. Chapter 4 helps define where to start the network automation journey.

Chapter 1 What is Network Automation?

"I am putting myself to the fullest possible use, which is all I think that any conscious entity can ever hope to do"
- **HAL 9000**

Network automation is the transformation of traditionally human performed functions, and human driven operations, to an automated engine that is data and machine driven. A fully automated network configuration management system is delivered through a development framework adhering to a strict System Development Lifecycle (SDLC). Network automation does not replace solid network designs or the need to understand basic network concepts such as what a VLAN is or what a routing protocol does. Network automation can be a tactical one-time change across the enterprise, for example, standardizing the native Network Time Protocol (NTP) server or making sure every network device has a banner displayed at login time. Network automation can also be complete configuration coverage where the entire running-configuration is derived from, and automatically generated by, the automation engine. This moves the network to an intent-driven model with a real source of truth – the code repository. The new methodology for making changes now includes a centralized repository, branching strategy, committing changes, and performing pull requests to merge approved code into a protected master branch. The full potential of network automation is achieved when developers update an intent-based, source of truth repository. Changes are then automatically documented, tested, and released to the network through a continuous integration / continuous delivery (CI/CD) pipeline.

Traditional Legacy Network Management

For better and for worse, one of the great things about networks is that, for the most part, not a lot has changed over the past 30 years. The OSI model was published in 1984 and yes, there has been a lot of function virtualization, bigger and faster boxes, and improvements in bandwidth, but once an administrator has learned to operate a device, along with the fundamentals of networking and the OSI model, configuring and operating the network becomes predictable and a somewhat tedious task. While the size and scale of modern networks has exploded, few tools have emerged to operate and configure network devices at scale. Connecting to the CLI and applying configurations manually device-by-device, line-by-line, regardless of the scale, has long been the only methodology available to network administrators. Modern network management systems do exist as appliances or specialized software; however, many do not offer much more beyond a GUI representing the line-by-line commands. Even more painful is ensuring that network documentation is up to date if it exists at all. In some cases, a real source of truth about the network may not exist. The network running-configurations device-to-device may itself be the source of truth.

This method of running a network guarantees that human errors will be made. Any number of problems can occur from fat fingers, bad copy-paste, order of operations problems, sometimes even being on the wrong device! Mistakes will happen as long we rely on manual changes. Network automation allows the team to focus on higher level tasks while relying on the automation engine to perform the functions that are prone to human error. Administrators will still play a vital role making valuable contributions to the operation of the network. With the tools introduced in this book operators can augment their abilities with the powerful automation engine and do what was previously impossible.

Consider today's typical network change workflow:

- A new project has network requirements or changes are required to the network.
- An administrator collects the data, possibly from multiple devices, often manually, to assess the current network state to draft the change.
- The change might first need to be developed and tested in a non-production environment or an impact assessment might need to be performed if the change is deemed disruptive.
- Configuration commands are developed.
- Once tested and ready, changes are submitted into a ticketing system and assigned to a network operator.
- The operator reviews the change artifacts and implements the change manually by following a series of instructions.
- Pre and post-change information is gathered to validate the change. This often takes a substantial amount of time and will be point-in-time information.

If things do not go well or mistakes happen, it is often difficult to identify the root cause or confirm the operator followed the correct steps error-free. Problems caused by a change are usually discovered because of an outage. Ideally, network monitoring system alarms are triggered but in a worst-case scenario, it is a user who reports the issue. Manual troubleshooting and problem resolution is necessary as well as manual updates of all relevant and affected documentation. Network automation solves all these problems while drastically reducing the time and effort involved in gathering information, resolving problems, and deploying changes to the network.

Aside from safe, pre-approved changes, the majority of network configuration changes occur after business hours. Several network administrators may be required to perform changes manually at a larger scale or a longer change window may be required by a smaller team. By automating solutions, the organization can dramatically reduce outage windows as well as the operator hours required to implement changes. Changes that previously took hours of execution time can now be performed in seconds.

The drawbacks and problems inherited by the tools such as a console cable, Telnet, SSH sessions, and a keyboard have impeded the progress of modern networks, especially at scale. Putty session copy-paste only goes so far. A lot of Network Management Systems (NMS) have emerged from both hardware vendors and third-party companies trying to fill the need for better network management tools. However, due to the huge number of features an NMS must offer (monitoring, reporting, configuration management, provisioning, capacity, utilization and performance statistics) large NMS systems tend to do a lot of things well but nothing great. Intent-based solutions are only starting to emerge as appliances or software and are only capable of delivering solutions for a single vendor. NMS solutions involve licensing and can become costly as the network scales. Most NMS require training to be fully leveraged and are often underutilized by an organization either due to a lack of the NMS's ability to provide solutions or the complexity of being able to build solutions in the NMS.

Operational Challenges

Many challenges exist with the legacy approach to managing networks either through CLI device-to-device or through complicated, expensive, NMS solutions that still require a great deal of CLI work.

The following is a brief list of key problems inherent to the legacy approach:

- No source of truth.
  - Networks often lack a source of truth: an authoritative artifact that can be referenced for what the desired working configuration of a device or set of devices is.

- Often decentralized in project folders, file shares, Visio diagrams, Excel spreadsheets, and local drives.
- Sometimes the network itself **is** the source of truth: the running-configurations of each device is the only source of information about the network.

- Documentation.
  - Documentation tends to fall out of date and requires manual updates when changes are made to the network.
  - Often missed or overlooked.
  - Often decentralized.
  - Rarely referenced by network operators due to above complications.

- Scale.
  - Networks are not getting smaller. Internet of Things (IoT), wireless access points, IP phones, rapid WAN expansion, cloud adoption, and larger data centers are leading to massive enterprise networks.
  - CLI simply does not scale unless more people are added to manage the network.

- Error-prone.
  - Mistakes happen with manual changes.
  - Requires orchestration of complex changes ensuring the correct order of device and command entry.
  - Requires work to be done several times per change. Plan, document, submit, and implement into production.
  - Sometimes approval processes or operational mistakes occur where changes are completed out of order from when they were submitted, causing overwrites or outages.

- Large-scale changes.
  - Deployment of new features often takes a very long time because of scale or complexity.
  - New business requirements and device types connecting to the network may require QoS policy changes leading to rewrite the QoS policy for every device.
  - Some changes are avoided because the effort required to make a correction or deploy a feature is too great.

- Limitations of available alternatives.
  - Aside from CLI or an NMS there are very few alternatives to managing a network.
  - Newer, intent-based solutions have only recently emerged with little proven capability.

- Talent.
  - The complexity of networks has grown along with their size and scale. Virtualization, multicast, QoS, STP, routing, routing protocols, cloud, security, firewalls, wireless, voice, video, VSS, HSRP, VPN, 802.1x, along with increasingly complicated commands to gather information.
  - Staffing challenges such as finding certified IT staff or expanding network operations head count. Every change to the network becomes a challenge as the complexity increases.

- Cost.
  - Downtime and change window requirements.
  - Overtime requirements.

o   Large network operations staffing requirements.

Software-Defined Networking

Before discussing Software-Defined Networking (SDN), some basic networking concepts will be introduced. Theoretically, there are three planes in computer networks: the management plane; the control plane; and the data plane.

Management Plane

Human Operator / Tools Managing Network Devices

CLI, SNMP, REST-API, NETCONF

Control Plane

Protocol exchanges with state information

OSPF, EIGRP, BGP, RIP

Data plane

Movement of data packets; Network traffic

Routing tables, MAC address-tables

SDN, also affectionately known as "Still Does Nothing", aims to separate and centralize the control plane functions of the network while leaving the data plane functions distributed amongst the devices. The management plane functionality, however, remains distributed and still requires, even under SDN, at least some device-to-device management. SDN has not exactly been the silver bullet magically solving all organizational challenges faced with operating a large-scale network. However, SDN has been given new life, particularly for decoupling and centralizing the management plane in the form of network automation. The focus of this book is to show how Ansible can be used to interface with the management plane.

* Important note *: any control plane or data plane configurations used in this book are intended to be purely educational examples, not functional network designs, and have been derived from a fictional virtual network.

Introduction to Network Automation

Network automation, at its core, is the conversion of networks from a collection of independent configurations and transforming them into a unified application. Applications are written as code in certain programming languages, compiled, and then executed. Application developers around the world use a proven set of methodologies and best practices for software development. A key concept and component of network automation is the conversion of network configurations to code.

Network automation exists in many forms using a wide variety of technologies and it means different things to different people. For this book, network automation is the ability to abstract data from network configurations while using a machine to push commands and templated configurations to network devices securely, agentless, and at any scale, through a CI/CD pipeline.

Information about the network is often gathered through traditional Simple Network Management Protocol (SNMP) protocols combined with NMS solutions. SNMP provides a wealth of information about the network but is often limited to health monitoring of a device on the network. Most of the information about the logical network is gathered using **show** commands input by network operators or engineers at the CLI. Gathering information from the network is time consuming because these commands are nearly impossible to configure an NMS that is required in order to execute and gather output, especially at scale.

What if a network engineer wanted to gather all the Cisco Discovery Protocol (CDP) neighbors on the network to confirm a topology? Or confirm the spanning-tree information from each device to build a layer 2 topology of the network? What about gathering routing table information to build a layer 3 topology? What if the system could gather all the Open Shortest Path First (OSPF) neighbors? What if the current IOS version of every device on the network could be collected without an NMS? Gathering this information takes a lot of manual effort using traditional network management solutions. Utilizing network automation, network administrators craft Ansible playbooks to perform these tasks by building an on-demand library of utilities.

The best part about this approach is that it is completely non-disruptive and non-intrusive to the network. Operators are gathering information from the network while developing programming skills and learning the new workflow. At the same time, they are starting to understand the new processes and tools involved in network automation such as:

- Begin using TFS:
    - o Work items are created to identify, assign, and track progress on code development.
    - o Distributed teams are able to easily collaborate on shared work items.
    - o A centralized repository containing the Ansible playbooks as well as the resulting output starts to evolve.

- Implement a branching strategy:
    - o A single, authoritative master branch represents the known working state and configuration of the network.
    - o The master branch is protected. Changes are never made directly to the master branch.

- o A working branch per change is created. Developers perform Git commits often within a working branch.
  - o Approved pull requests are used to merge tested code from working branches into the master branch.

- Version control is established on information gathering Ansible playbooks:
  - o In concert with the branching strategy version control becomes apparent.
  - o As Ansible playbooks are refactored over time TFS will contain the change and version history.
  - o In addition to Ansible development skills, operators start to familiarize themselves with Git.

- Playbook library:
  - o Network engineers can work with the network operations team to find the most common manual commands used for network reconnaissance.
  - o These commands are transformed into automated playbooks that operations can start using to troubleshoot or gather information from the network.
  - o Working playbooks are easily cloned, refactored, and added to the library by operators or engineers.

Building on these principals, the organization starts to gradually embrace network automation without risk. The power unlocked will become evident immediately and the organization can start considering a wider scale adoption and automating changes to the network. Chapter 6 contains more details and concrete examples that can be used on the network today.

There is always risk associated with making changes to the network. Despite the best designs and architectures some changes are disruptive, and outages cannot be avoided. Networks also have the largest blast radius in the enterprise. The scope of change impact increases the closer to the network core changes are made. For example, an entire building can be isolated from the network if changes cause an outage at the distribution layer. If the network is down, almost every other aspect of the organization is impacted in some way. Uptime is of the utmost importance to an organization because of the business impact network downtime can cause. These factors can lead to an extremely risk adverse view of network operations. The less change the better.

The biggest challenge in network automation is an organization's willingness to adopt it. Despite obvious benefits, which become clear throughout this book, there can be a lot of resistance to this type of revolutionary change, particularly regarding changes to the network. This mindset is also at odds with the modern pressures and business demands of the network to be, ironically, constantly changing. Network automation is in fact a safer and more reliable approach, partly because it all but eliminates manual error.

Making one-time, tactical configuration changes is a great place to move from automating network reconnaissance to automating changes to the network. A one-time change to the network or a tactical configuration change is something that will be done once and is throw away work. These are often tedious jobs when performed manually at scale. Oversites in design may be found in production leading to required corrections. Perhaps legacy code has become deprecated and needs to be replaced. Maybe standards or conventions were not followed leading to a non-golden configuration. Net-new requirements, for example a new Dynamic Host Configuration Protocol (DHCP) server, will frequently arise during normal day-to-day operations. Every organization is different, and each network is going to have unique requirements and challenges. Here are some opportunities for tactical, one-time changes that can be automated:

- Application of standards or conventions:
  - o This can be a standard Network Time Protocol (NTP) server for all network devices or ensuring the native VLAN is set correctly on all trunk ports.

- Correcting errors:
  - o If there are known problems on the network that have been put off because of the scale of the change, lack of priority, tedium, understanding of the amount of manual effort required, lack of resources, or waiting for an automated solution to arrive.

- Net-new projects:
  - o Draw a line in the sand and try to commit to automating all net-new project requirements that require changes to the network.

As part of the repository, have a place for one-time tactical Ansible playbooks. These playbooks will become part of the larger network automation framework and are available for cloning and repurposing. Examples of successful plays helps others develop their own playbooks and code. Chapter 7 has several use cases of one-time tactical plays that can be used as a foundation to solve unique challenges.

At this point the organization should be comfortable with using network automation for information collection and making changes to the network. While these are both great capabilities that will completely change network operations, the real power of network automation is full configuration management coverage. Every device is configured by the network automation engine using dynamic templates powered by abstracted data models. Essentially, converting the network configurations to code. This code is intent-driven data models in human-readable format, comprised of variables and dynamic templates that contain the configurations. Version control can now be implemented using Git. The compiled configurations are then pushed to the network through automated Ansible playbooks. Chapter 8 covers this in more detail.

Creating a CI/CD pipeline is the last step to fully automating the network. Automated builds, tests and releases are now available to network operations. As part of the branching strategy, builds can be triggered automatically whenever pull requests merge code into the master branch (CI). Releases can be scheduled and deployed to the network much like a patch to software is released to applications. Scheduled releases can occur at any frequency – hourly, nightly, weekly, monthly. Approved changes are merged into the master branch in the repository which automatically triggers the deployment during the next scheduled release (CD). This is the full power of network automation unleashed.

Impact on IT

The impact on IT should not be underestimated. There is a lot of change and learning involved. It is not just the tools or new file types or data formats, but the very mindset of IT itself, which can be very hard to change. Acceptance of innovation often faces risk adversity and a natural resistance to change. Network automation will absolutely lead to changes in core processes for change management and network operations. Network maintenance will be automated, and this could mean some restructuring or refocusing of staff.

The only thing that can break network automation is manual intervention and therefore it is imperative that everyone involved with the network fully understands and is onboard with the new direction and processes. Manual changes are in direct contrast with intent-based networks and will be overwritten by the automation solutions. That said, a balance must be struck. In an emergency the CLI will never be replaced, however be sure to track all out of band changes applied to fix the issue. Retroactively include these changes in the code repository as an out of band emergency branch. All the manual emergency changes should be captured and incorporated into the repository.

NetDevOps

NetDevOps builds on the DevOps model from the application world but is applied to the networking functions of an organization. The network "developers" (senior network engineers, architects, designers) and the network "operators" (network administrators, network support staff, day-to-day network operations) are blended under a new framework. The senior developers are empowered to deliver into production directly through release management using pull requests. The operations team updates the data models and executes playbooks for routine network changes. Operations most likely will not write or update the dynamic templates. Templates will be developed by the senior network staff. In the case of NetDevOps benefits can be found by having software developers join this new team to help create the data models and templates with the input from the network team. Blending IT and blurring the lines can lead to questions of where authorized changes come from. Fortunately, the automation engine itself is making the changes. Approvals should now look like peer reviews of code and traditional quality assurance (QA) as changes are now code based.

The impact to network operators is tangible. Operators learn to write playbooks to help run the network, identify problems, and troubleshoot. Most network changes will be automated to much easier tasks such as running an Ansible playbook as a single line command. Using the features available in TFS, operations now has version control available in the form of pull requests and Git commit information. Change approvals are built directly into the pipeline allowing for automated delivery of solutions.

Skills

Converting the network team into a development shop takes time, practice, training and support from the organization. Staff will continue to require essential network training while learning and developing their programming skills. The code itself will improve over time as skills are polished. Code is easily refactored once better methods or improved logic develops. The best way to improve these new skills is, ideally, to try and fully automate a lab environment if one is available. Having a lab environment where staff can safely troubleshoot allows them to develop without fear of causing an impact to production. Code should only interact with a production environment after it has been fully vetted, and the effects of the implementation understood. Once the code is fully tested in a safe environment, it can be ported over to the production environment worry-free.

Tools

The standard network administrator toolkit is not fully replaced. Network administration still includes:

- Putty or an SSH session manager to get to the CLI.
- NMS systems that may already be in place (Cisco Prime Infrastructure, Nagios, etc.).
- IOS commands and configurations.
- Existing skills on the CLI.

However, the toolkit now includes:

- Microsoft Visual Studio Code (VS Code).
- Microsoft Team Foundation Server (TFS).
- Linux.
- Git.
- Ansible.
- A central code repository in TFS.
- A local code repository for development in VS Code.
- A local code repository on the Linux / Ansible host to execute playbooks.
- A master branch.
- Working branches.
- A **hosts.ini** file.
- Data models (Ansible **group_vars** and **host_vars**, YAML files holding variables).
- Dynamic templates.
- Tasks.
- Playbooks.
- The YAML file format and syntax.
- The Jinja2 file format and syntax.
- Python skills, ideally, but not required for Ansible beginners.

Converting Configurations to Code

The goal is to transform the network from a series of interconnected but unrelated and independently configured devices, to a holistic application-like system. Start by collecting relevant data from the existing network. Abstract meaningful data from the configurations and then convert that data into a model. The network should follow a standard core, distribution, and access layer architecture. A solid IP address plan should already exist, and the network should follow some basic conventions and standards. If the network is built on these foundations, converting it to code should be quite simple.

It should be noted that if the network is chaotic in nature and lacks basic standards it may be easier to start from scratch and approach it as a greenfield. Standards and conventions can be enforced using automation. Start by developing models and templates and address the lack of standards on the network as a starting point. Remember garbage-in, garbage-out.

If the network is relatively standardized, collect the running-configurations from the core, a distribution switch, and an access switch. Try to find devices that represent a standard deployment that can be modeled after and templated from. Extract and separate the important information from the configuration commands. The important information will become variables that go into data models and the configuration commands will go into templates. Meaningful data can include:

- Standard global configuration information:
  - AAA information.
  - QoS policies.
  - SNMP information.
  - Logging information.
  - NTP information.
  - Archive information.

- Hostname.

- VLAN information.
- SVI information.
- VRF information.
- Routing (OSPF, EIGRP, static routes) information.
- Default gateway.
- Access control lists.
- Physical and virtual interface standards:
  - VLAN.
  - IP Address.
  - Voice VLAN.
  - STP toolkit settings.
  - Power over Ethernet (PoE) settings.
  - QoS settings.
  - 802.1x or port security settings.
  - Trunk or access port settings.

Data Models

Data models are structured, human-readable, intent-based text files. Data models are also known as data dictionaries and hold the variables leveraged by dynamic templates. These models become the source of truth and network devices are configured to a desired state based on intent. Data models are written in YAML format. For the most part key-pair values and lists make up a data model. There will be both group and host variables that apply to a collection of devices or an individual device on the network. Modeling data is a key component of network automation and considerable time and care should be spent creating them. It is not uncommon to refactor a model multiple times before the most effective way to handle data that can scale is found.

Here is a sample data model, in YAML format, for a campus access switch:

```
---

host_defaults:
  hostname: ACCESS01
  stack_size: 2
  site: 10
  snmp_engineid: 1001
  snmp_server_location: "Building01_FirstFloor"

host_vlans:
  2:
   name: "In-BandManagement"

  3:
   name: WirelessAccessPoints

  10:
   name: BLUE_Zone

  11:
   name: BLUE_Zone_Voice

  20:
```

```
    name: RED_Zone

  30:
   name: GREEN_Zone

  50:
   name: SECURITY


host_virtual_interfaces:
  Vlan2:
   description: "In-BandManagement"
   ip_address: "192.168.1.1 255.255.255.0"
   state_enabled: true

host_port_channels:
  Port-channel1:
   port_channel: 1
   description: "Distribution Uplink"
   encapsulation: dot1q
   switchport_mode: trunk
   switchport_nonegotiate: true
   vlans: 2,3,10,11,20,30,50
   state_enabled: true
   members:
     GigabitEthernet1/0/48:
       power_inline: false
       srr_queue_share: true
       srr_queue_shape: true
       priority_queue: out
       trust_dscp: true
       lacp: active
       service_policy:
         input: QoS-IN
       state_enabled: true

     GigabitEthernet2/0/48:
       power_inline: false
       srr_queue_share: true
       srr_queue_shape: true
       priority_queue: out
       trust_dscp: true
       lacp: active
       service_policy:
         input: QoS-IN
       state_enabled: true

host_interfaces:
  GigabitEthernet1/0/1:
   type: OPZone
   description: Standard OPZone Interface
   vlan: 10
   voice_vlan: 11
   state_enabled: true


  GigabitEthernet1/0/2:
```

```
type: SECURITY
description: Standard Security Interface
vlan: 50
state_enabled: true
```

Templates

Templates are human-readable Jinja2 files made up of logical operators, dynamic variables and static text. Once combined with group and host variables each device receives a unique configuration derived from and based on the dynamic templates. The spacing of the text, syntax and unique platform variations of text all need to match a device's running-configuration. Templates ensure that intentions are defined and that golden configurations on all devices adhere to the standards.

Here is a sample template, in the Jinja2 format, to configure VLANs on a device:

```
vlan {{ global_campus_defaults.native_vlan }}
 name NativeVLAN

{% if host_vlans is defined %}
{%     for host_vlan in host_vlans %}
vlan {{ host_vlan }}
 name {{ host_vlans[host_vlan].name }}
{%     endfor %}
{% endif %}
```

Methodology

Some of the biggest changes that network automation brings is the new methodology available now that the network has become application-like and is comprised of standard human-readable code. Instead of network engineers drafting configuration changes and network operations deploying to production at the CLI, they can follow a CI/CD pipeline with change management, version control and a branching strategy. Documentation will move to TFS as it becomes automated along with the configurations of the devices. Reviewing pull requests and Git commits will become part of the routine for network engineers as they peer review and approve changes to the master branch. The SDLC approach to software development should already exist in the organization. An opportunity exists to bridge IT with software development which adopts already existing code standards and development policies for the new network automation code. Initially, network engineers will write Ansible playbooks that operations will execute as a one-line command at an approved schedule. Eventually these steps become automated through the CI/CD pipeline.

Network Development Lifecycle (NDLC)

A network development lifecycle can be adopted to help provide a high-level vision and guidance around network development. A framework for the branch structure is required. Developers need to perform Git commits frequently checking-in their code often. A common data model format needs to be:

- Followed uniformly by all developers.
- Naming conventions established.
- Standardized templates and programmatic code formats developed.
- Code should include comments.

A formalized pull request structure, including documentation, testing requirements, and an overall approval process, is the foundation for merging code from development into production.

Create the build (CI) and release (CD) pipeline structure. Small feature releases and pre-approved changes can be merged into the master branch quickly and easily. The code change will be delivered automatically when the next scheduled release occurs. Disruptive changes, larger changes, and major feature releases should all require approvals and be scheduled in advance especially larger one-time releases. Schedule these changes outside of the regular release cycle depending on urgency.

Many traditional NDLCs directly translate to network automation code development strategies. The "Prepare, Plan, Design, Implement, Operate, Optimize" (PPDIOO) methodology from Cisco, for example, nicely fits the network automation vision laid out in this book. The same lifecycle approach to network infrastructure should be applied to the new network automation code. The first steps (prepare, plan, design) are performed in VS Code while Ansible is used to perform the implement and operate steps. Refactoring code can be considered the optimization stage of the lifecycle.

For more on PPDIOO please visit:

http://www.ciscopress.com/articles/article.asp?p=1608131&seqNum=3

Ansible

Ansible was written by Michael DeHaan and developed by the Ansible Community, Ansible Inc., and Red Hat Inc. Initially released on February 20, 2012, Ansible's latest stable version as of the writing of this book is 2.7.0.

According to the Red Hat whitepaper "Ansible in Depth" the design goals for Ansible were:

- Minimal in nature.
- Consistent.
- Secure.
- Highly reliable.
- Minimal learning required.

https://www.ansible.com/resources/whitepapers/ansible-in-depth/

Another important distinguishing feature is that Ansible is agentless. SSH is used to connect Ansible to network devices. Nothing requires configuration on the devices aside from standard CLI access and possibly a service account when using RSA or other forms of AAA authentication on the network. Aside from Ansible needing to login to the device there are no other requirements to the network. Ansible is also cross platform across Linux, Windows, UNIX, F5 (BIG-IP) and Cisco network device OS (IOS, NX-OS).

Ansible by Red Hat is the open source version and Red Hat Ansible Engine is the commercially available version. Ansible is an automation engine that runs playbooks written in YAML format. Tasks are executed serially and offer full orchestration control within a playbook.

Framework

Think of Ansible more as an automation framework rather than a programming language. Ansible is not C++ or Java for networks but rather a framework of tools made up of the following:

- Inventory:
  - Static **hosts.ini** file.
  - Possibly dynamic using API calls to NMS, IPAM, or inventory system already maintained with a list of network devices.

- Variables:
  - **group_vars**.
  - **host_vars**.
  - YAML format.
  - Data models for network devices as a group and as individual devices.

- Playbooks:
  - YAML file format.
  - Serial execution of tasks.
  - Calls Ansible modules.

- Templates:
  - Jinja2 file format.
  - Dynamic calls to the variables at playbook run time.
  - Mix of static text, simple logic ("if", "else", "for"), and variables.

- Plug-ins:
  - Python format.
  - Extend base capabilities of core Ansible engine.
  - Custom written.

- Modules:
  - Python and PowerShell format.
  - Vendor specific modules for communicating with devices.

Python

Python (*https://www.python.org/*) is a powerful, easy to learn, open source programming language and is the foundation for Ansible. Created by Guido van Rossum and released in 1991 Python has a design philosophy of readability. The Ansible repository is available at GitHub (*https://github.com/ansible/ansible/*) and it is possible to contribute to the community project. While it is not necessary to understand the Python code Ansible is written in, it is possible to write Ansible plug-ins using Python or contribute code to the Ansible project once Python is well understood.

YAML

YAML Ain't Markup Language (*http://yaml.org/*) (*https://github.com/yaml/*) is a human-readable data serialization language commonly used for configuration files. YAML was created by Clark Evans who designed it together with Ingy döt Net and Oren Ben-Kiki in 2001. Most of the Ansible files, including group and host variables, tasks, and playbooks are written in YAML format. VS Code has YAML extensions to help write proper YAML code while modeling the network or writing Ansible playbooks.

Jinja2

Jinja2 (*http://jinja.pocoo.org/*) (*https://github.com/pallets/jinja/*), created by Armin Ronacher in 2008, is a full featured templating engine for Python. Ansible templates will be written in Jinja2 syntax. Templates are made up of a combination of static text, dynamic variables, and programmatic logic.

Playbooks

Ansible playbooks are written in YAML. Playbooks are executed against devices in the inventory file. For full configuration management, it is required that group variables, host variables, templates, and tasks be developed in addition to the inventory file. To run an Ansible playbook, execute the following command in the Linux host:

```
ansible-playbook <filename.yml>
```

Idempotency

Idempotency is a key feature of Ansible. To be idempotent means the same task can be executed a single or multiple (infinite) times and the results will always be the same. To say the network is idempotent means the source of truth (including the results from the Ansible playbook), and the running-configuration of a device, match when compared. Once idempotent, Ansible playbooks will show the results of the playbook in green text, indicating no changes will be made because the two configurations are identical. If the configurations are not idempotent, the Ansible playbook will show a change in yellow text, reporting a change will be made by the playbook.

By reaching full coverage of the network configurations and transforming the configurations to code the master branch becomes a full representation of the network. All future changes become extremely easy to validate using the branching strategy of a working branch per change. These working branches can be executed in check mode.

Check Mode

Ansible playbooks have a check mode where playbooks can be tested without executing any changes. The combination of idempotency and check mode is very powerful.

Ideally:

- Make code change.
- Run code in check mode with verbosity enabled.
- Confirm exact change reflected in output of check mode.
- Run code in execute mode.
- Re-run play in check mode to confirm play results are in green text indicating no changes will be made and that the automated configuration matches the running-configuration.

Automating a mistake can arguably lead to faster impact, on a larger scale, then a mistake made manually at the CLI (a single device). For something as potentially dangerous as network automation in such a risk adverse field, check mode offers the ability to perform a dry run of a playbook without making any modifications to the network. Check mode, on its own, will show hosts in green text indicating no changes would have been made by the Ansible playbook if it was executed. Should changes be found the hosts with changes will show in yellow text. This indicates Ansible, in execute mode, would have pushed changes to the device. It also indicates the playbook is not idempotent. Results can be documented and included as artifacts in the change management approval process. Stress is reduced, and reassurance is offered further easing the transition to network automation. For all changes that cannot be performed in a lab environment or for large disruptive changes touching many devices, check mode can be used to show the exact commands the playbook will execute serially device-by-device.

```
ansible-playbook <playbook.yml> --check
```

Differentials

Differentials (`-- diff`) are another option for Ansible playbooks. Diff is often used in conjunction with check mode. If the Ansible module supports diff, playbooks can be executed with the option set to compare the automated configuration against the device's configuration. This is useful for before and after comparisons or to fully understand the changes the playbook would have made had it been running in execute mode.

```
ansible-playbook <playbook.yml> --diff
```

Or when combined with check mode and verbosity:

```
ansible-playbook <playbook.yml --check –diff -v
```

A detailed guide "Check Mode ("Dry Run")" is available here:

https://docs.ansible.com/ansible/latest/user_guide/playbooks_checkmode.html

Verbosity

Various levels of verbosity can be set when running the playbooks to provide more details in the output from the playbook. When combined with check mode, for example, adding one level of verbosity will show potential changes in yellow text and will also output the exact text of the configurations that would be changed. Deeper levels of verbosity exist providing even more granular output. This is useful for troubleshooting playbooks.

Tags

Tags can be added to tasks within a playbook. This can help organize, group or classify tasks and is very useful for larger playbooks. Tagged tasks can be run inside a larger playbook. Conversely it is possible to run all tasks except the tagged tasks. Tags are a way to provide meta data and organizational structure to tasks.

A detailed guide to Ansible tags is available here:

https://docs.ansible.com/ansible/2.6/user_guide/playbooks_tags.html

A guide to Ansible playbooks is available here:

https://docs.ansible.com/ansible/2.7/cli/ansible-playbook.html

Ansible Tower

Ansible Tower is a commercially available, GUI-based, playbook orchestration system that provides the ability to scale network automation solutions to even larger deployments. Role-Based Access Control (RBAC), playbook scheduling, reporting, and inventory management are all key components of Ansible Tower. Ansible Tower can make the integration of Ansible in the organization easier as it provides a more familiar GUI-based approach and includes some key components most organizations require such as RBAC, reporting, and playbook scheduling. Ansible Tower can also be integrated into the TFS CI/CD pipeline. An open source version, AWX, is available.

More information about Ansible Tower can be found here:

https://www.ansible.com/products/tower/

https://docs.ansible.com/#tower

More information about AWX can be found here:

https://www.ansible.com/products/awx-project/faq/

Source Control

After a successful transition from a collection of configurations to code, source control needs to be implemented. The organization's development team likely has source control implemented which can be leveraged along with best practices and processes for changes to source code. Source control is a vital component of the new NDLC for network engineers and operations.

Treating the network as code implies strong source controls. Network configurations stored as code benefit greatly from these source controls as the given state of the network, or individual components of the network, is known at all times. Changes that are tracked using source control display the exact changes and the pre-change / post-change state of the network devices intended configuration. Strong source control means when problems occur on the network, answering the standard "what changed?" question is extremely easy to figure out.

Git

Git is a free, open source, and distributed version control system created by Linus Torvalds in 2005 for development of the Linux kernel. Consider Git the glue that holds the NDLC lifecycle together tracking all changes to files using commits. These tracked changes are included in the history of all Git repositories and changes can be rolled back to any point-in-time.

Microsoft Team Foundation Server (TFS)

"Share code. Track work. Ship software" is Microsoft's slogan for TFS. TFS is "the integrated server suite of developer tools for professional teams" providing advanced source code management. TFS covers the entire application lifecycle and can be used to develop automated builds and scheduled releases thus creating the CI/CD pipeline. TFS features include: work center, code repositories, build, test, and release capabilities. TFS has native Git support and Ansible extensions are available in the Microsoft Marketplace.

Work

TFS has a dynamic work center for cross team collaboration and item tracking. As new changes, feature requirements, or code refactoring needs arise, work items can be added to the board. Using this centralized repository members of cross functional teams can be assigned, track progress, or complete work items. Working branches can be created directly from these work items allowing code development to begin immediately and then tracked for status.

Code

Repositories are kept under TFS code along with a file explorer, branch explorer, repository history and pull request information. It is recommended to keep natural network environments in separate repositories (lab, production, development). Branches are available for comparison and tracking versions. Pull requests have an entire workflow capability and are used to merge working branches into the master branch. RBAC and approvals for pull requests into the master branch should be implemented. The master branch should be protected in TFS, thus preventing direct development in this branch, further enforcing the strategy.

Continuous Integration / Continuous Delivery (CI/CD)

In the context of network automation, continuous integration (CI) and continuous delivery (CD) implies full network automation of tasks. This pipeline should be abstracted as an orchestrated chain of automated actions and events based on intent. Through the build – test – release cycle, CI/CD can be achieved. CI enables distributed software development across many teams. Small but frequent incremental changes are continuously integrated into the master branch. CD then automatically deploys these changes to the production network.

Build

A build is a software product in its final, consumable form. While builds are not a necessary part of using Ansible for network automation, they can be used to perform CI/CD. When creating a build in TFS Ansible playbooks can be executed as tasks as part of the build. Network reconnaissance playbooks, are completely harmless to execute automatically, and can run every time a pull request merges code into the master branch. Pull requests can trigger automated builds which in turn trigger Ansible playbooks. This is the CI in the CI/CD pipeline.

Automated testing can be triggered by the automated build. Builds can be deployed to test specific lab environments, a Virl environment or a Jenkins environment. Unlike software which can easily be tested in virtual environments, depending on the environment, network testing may not apply to network automation playbooks. Instead testing could be incorporated directly into an Ansible playbook. Be aware of the automated testing TFS offers.

For more information about Cisco Virl please visit:

http://virl.cisco.com/

For more information about Jenkins please visit:

https://jenkins.io/

Release

Releasing software, in this case network configurations, is driven by Ansible playbooks as the final step in the CI/CD pipeline. Builds can be scheduled or triggered by pull requests. Ansible playbooks can be built into the release steps in TFS. While highly exciting, automated releases should be carefully considered and performed with a full understanding of the impact of the change. Disruptive changes may require specially coordinated releases while routine pre-approved changes can be continuously delivered in real-time. Check mode, documentation playbooks, automated testing playbooks and reviewing commits in the pull request are all validation steps and quality assurances used to ensure the CI/CD pipeline does not have unintended consequences.

There can be great reluctance to move to a full CI/CD pipeline with fully automated changes being made to the production network. After all, if great care is not taken in developing, testing, retesting and documenting code, a mistake can be automated, possibly taking down the network. However, when successfully implemented, automation using a CI/CD pipeline can transform an organization's entire approach to designing and operating the enterprise network. This is a revolutionary opportunity!

Summary

For years enterprise class networks have been waiting for a scalable solution to basic network configuration management. Networks continue to be the bottleneck in IT service delivery and the root cause of many outages and downtime partly because of the lack of management tools available. Networks continue to require large specialized support teams and many lack relevant documentation. Networks have not evolved alongside the other moving parts of organizations. Software defined networking attempted to segregate and centralize the network control plane, while leaving the data plane decentralized across the network. While this approach did not necessarily take hold and transform the industry, the idea of decoupling the networking planes and centralizing the management plane has found great success using network automation.

Network automation can be understood simply as the conversion of network configurations to software-like application code including the tools, methodologies and processes used by the software development discipline. Every aspect of the traditional enterprise network can be automated using a modern network development lifecycle (NDLC) powered by an automation engine - Ansible. Ultimately the goal is to reach a continuous integration / continuous delivery (CI/CD) pipeline. Code changes are made by developers, using pull requests, which merges code into the repository's master branch. A series of orchestrated automated tasks, such as change validation, documentation generation, and delivery to production, is in turn kicked off.

Chapter 2 Why Automate the Network?

"The remains of the old must be decently laid away; the path of the new prepared. That is the difference between Revolution and Progress."
- Henry Ford

The time for change has arrived. Enterprise networks have outgrown and outpaced the ability to effectively manage and maintain themselves using traditional tools. Historically, network management meant manually gathering point-in-time information from, or making configuration changes to, individual devices. Networks are often designed using a configuration command-driven approach, as opposed to a data-driven approach. Staff manually execute commands at the CLI to gather information or perform changes. Information is often regathered to confirm the state of the network after changes are made. The ongoing creation and maintenance of network documentation is also performed manually. Hours of effort is required to make changes, often repeating the same commands only on different devices. Inevitably, troubleshooting is required because of errors made using the manual methodology. Network automation solves all these problems.

Scale

The size and scale of the modern network has grown exponentially to accommodate the needs of organizations. Networks that started out as a few switches and a router are now large-scale enterprise networks. While logical networks evolve and grow, the tools used to manage physical devices remains stagnant. On the campus we now see VoIP phones, wireless access points, IoT, security cameras, print fleets, desktop fleets and meeting room equipment. In the data centers large physical and virtual footprints are not uncommon. World-wide WANs, with switching and routing in each remote office, is now common place. The device boom has not slowed with even more devices being added to networks without the appropriate centralized, automated, management solutions available.

Network management starts with the console cable and a local CLI. Remote access to the CLI over a management IP address must be enabled by the administrator. Now imagine network technicians still needing to go to the physical console of every device to manage it. It sounds unreasonable, but only remote access to the CLI has been centralized. The same methodology of logging into the CLI to manage the device is followed as if the operator is virtually at the console. In fact, these remote connections are known as virtual teletype, or VTY, lines. At the scale of today's networks, connecting to the CLI of every device to manage the enterprise is simply unachievable. Even with a large capable network operations team, everyone is going to operate, configure, and manage each device their own way. This leads to configuration drift and a lack of consistency at scale.

Automated solutions scale with the network as device configurations are templated. Small, feature specific, modular templates ensures each device is standardized. When new feature requirements arise, the configuration commands are templated and released at scale, updating the network standards uniformly. Unique, device-specific, meaningful information is modeled in a data dictionary. This dictionary holds all the variables used to compile a unique configuration for each device. Code can be written modularly to match the topology of the network. By creating playbooks specific to the environment, such as campus, data center, WAN, or cloud, Ansible playbooks ensure code simplicity, readability and development flexibility.

Complexity

The complexity of networks has dramatically increased. Virtual Route Forwarders (VRFs), QoS, wireless connectivity, cloud connectivity, Virtual Private Network (VPN), First-Hop Redundancy Protocols (FHRP) such as Hot-Standby Router Protocol (HSRP), Virtual Switching Systems (VSS), and security and identity services such as 802.1x, have all stressed the capabilities of both engineers who design and operators who run the network.

Abstracting important data from the network configurations allows operators to see the network devices as a collection of human-readable variables and dynamic templates. This drastically simplifies network design. Human-readability of the intended configuration for a device also reduces the technical requirements needed to understand how a device is configured. The knowledge required to execute commands and understand how a device is configured is abstracted because the device information is presented as a human-readable data model.

Documentation

Network documentation is extremely important, especially during times of crisis, however it is often overlooked during day-to-day operations. Changes may or may not be reflected in documentation. Files may be scattered across a variety of sources such as local drives, Microsoft SharePoint sites, or network shares. Stale or out of date documentation is of little value to an organization. Documentation that does exist is often represented as complex Visio diagrams, large Excel spreadsheets or text files that do not interact with the network dynamically. Documentation should be thought of as a key component, and advantage, of the network automation solution. The scope of automation is not limited to making changes. Part of the TFS repository master branch should be a folder structure containing both the dynamic documentation Ansible playbooks, as well as folders for the generated output artifacts.

Automated documentation can be built directly into the CI/CD pipeline creating comma separated value (.csv), Markdown (.md), or text files. These files are then incorporated into Git commits and pull requests, becoming part of the code base and repository. TFS and VS Code can view these files natively, presenting a customizable view of the network as code. These artifacts include the intended, automatically generated, configuration files as well as the data model variables manipulated to express the information in different formats.

For example, is it possible to automatically generate the following documentation for each device, based on data model variables:

- VLANs.
- VRFs.
- Routing protocol configuration information.
- Static routes.
- Interface information:
    - Up / Down.
    - Mode – Access or Trunk.
    - VLAN(s).
- Port-channels information:
    - Member ports.
    - IP Addresses.
- Access Control Lists (ACL).

In fact, any information represented in a data model can be transformed into dynamic documentation files. This allows for desired information about any device on the network to be automatically generated at build time, and available through TFS. The history for these documentation files is included as source and version controls. When adding or removing code, the resulting documentation updates are automatically performed reflecting the changes.

Standards

Corporate standards are very hard to maintain over time as networks evolve and transform. Often the pressures of projects and deliverables of day-to-day work demands leads to standards being overlooked, put off, or ignored. Natural configuration drift can occur over time as network devices and IP addresses come and go. If network devices continue to operate, misconfigurations or poor standards may go unnoticed. When identified, these cosmetic corrections may be deemed a low priority.

Ansible's dynamic templating guarantees a standardized configuration for every device. Complete configuration coverage is achievable and every line of code in the running-configuration can be derived from a template. Having accomplished full idempotency between the source of truth and the device configuration guarantees intent-based standards are uniformly applied. Scale is not a problem with this approach nor is the human error factor. When new standards arise, or changes to existing standards are required, only the centralized templates and data models are updated. These changes are pushed through the automation engine delivering the new standards to the network.

Golden Configuration

Sometimes referred to in Windows operating system administration as a "desired state configuration" a golden configuration has many names. Using Jinja2 templates and YAML data models, a golden configuration for each device in the network is achieved using software development methodologies. Logic within the templates is used to intelligently generate device configuration commands. These configurations are applied at scale to all devices included in the Ansible **hosts.ini** inventory file.

The master branch represents the golden configuration for the network. Automated builds package the various artifacts from the master branch and provide a version number for that iteration of the network. When changes are required, however minor, working branches are created for code to be developed and tested. Frequent Git commits during development are used to check changes into the working branch. A pull request is used to merge these accumulated changes into the master branch, which is then deployed into production updating the standardized, golden configuration, at scale.

Security

Some of the largest security breaches occur because telnet is open on a port with a public facing IP address. Security standards and best practices can now be hard-coded into templates guaranteeing enforcement of policies. Often complex configurations are required on interfaces at the access layer to address security risks. Consider the access layer and all the following security standards that should be implemented:

- Spanning-tree toolkit commands.
  - o Bridge Protocol Data Unit (BPDU) controls.

- o Portfast.
- 802.1x or port-security commands.
- Data and voice VLANs.
- QoS settings.
- CDP settings.
- Power over Ethernet (PoE) settings.
- Native VLAN established.
- Native VLAN applied on trunk ports.
- NTP source.
- Security banner presented at login.
- AAA.
- RADIUS / TACACS+.
- ACLs on management ports.
- VLAN 1 disabled.

Security requirements, if missed or incorrectly applied, lead to vulnerabilities and threats within the network. These vulnerabilities can be exploited, lead to outages, or bring about data loss in certain scenarios. Having a guaranteed templated configuration ensures that important security components are hard-coded into every template and applied to both the device's global configuration as well as every interface configuration. Every access port throughout the campus can now be configured the same way and will automatically include security posture standards.

Agility

In an on-demand world networks continue to be the bottleneck of many projects. One of the driving factors for moving to automation is the agility it offers. Most of the common changes to the network become updates to existing data models. When new feature requirements arise, such as the need for multicast, new templates along with new data model variables will be developed. The feature is then released and incorporated into the orchestration of playbooks as a new task. A very repeatable, modular, process evolves which provides the agility to deliver projects more efficiently.

Design

Traditional network design often centers around the device configuration commands. While these commands are essential at implementation, it is the data that should drive network design. Network engineers' new responsibilities include crafting human-readable data models and the logic that drives the dynamic templates. Existing or new dynamic documentation should reflect new features as templates are added or updated. Thinking about data first, and the configuration second, network design evolves.

Deployment

The biggest advantages found in network automation are often on the operational side of network management. Large-scale changes are often very difficult to roll out to an enterprise. Introducing QoS to a network, for example, means touching all devices in all layers of the network, often with different code per platform. Devices using Multi-Layer Switching (MLS) or Modular Quality of Service Command Line (MQC) leads to different requirements and configuration commands by platform. Operations receives approved, finalized, network designs, along with deployment steps, from the network engineers. This often requires weeks or months to then complete the delivery to campus from start to end. Network automation, even a hybrid model where operators run Ansible playbooks manually, solves operational headaches related to deploying configurations to the network. Deployment time is drastically reduced when using Ansible playbooks while quality and accuracy significantly increases.

Operations

NetDevOps will dramatically change network operations' role in the organization. A library of canned, automated, Ansible playbooks develops over time. Automated builds and deployments will trigger whenever approved changes are merged into the repository. Operations are often tasked with running the network day-to-day, incorporating and deploying the changes coming from projects or network engineers. Operations will now learn to develop and use code.

If the deployment, network reconnaissance, and documentation aspects of operations can be automated, it will allow the operations team to focus on the day-to-day aspects of the network management along with new automated tools used to gather the information needed to run the network. With that said, the network may still have the need of an NMS for platform health monitoring. There may be network appliances or controllers that are not good candidates for automation or there may be non-SSH systems on the network that are non-automatable using Ansible.

Intent-Based

The human-readable nature of this methodology allows for a true intent-driven model of the network. The configurations are abstracted into the templates, so focus can be put on the data models. Intent for each device or group of devices can be expressed in a human-readable form. Idempotent Ansible playbooks combined with check mode can tell exactly if a device's running-configuration matches intent and if the Ansible playbook would have added code. Utilizing the differential option (`--diff`) allows the operator to see what differs between the two configurations and can also be displayed indicating any commands present on the device but missing from intent.

New appliance-based solutions are available that offer a GUI-driven intent system. Drag and drop intentions in the GUI are translated to configurations that are automatically pushed to the devices. These new intent-based appliances are the biggest competitor to Ansible network automation. Either purchase and configure the appliance, hoping it does everything advertised, or build an in-house Ansible automation framework.

Source of Truth

Every network should have an authoritative artifact identifying what is the correct, intended configuration for each device. Source of truth is a trusted artifact that network engineers and operators can reference with certainty. This can be an IP address, a static route, an ACL, or configuration command. It can be required when designing new solutions, adding new devices (scaling), troubleshooting problems, or rebuilding a device after failure.

Where is the network's source of truth? Is it a network management system? Flat files in folders in a network share? A Microsoft SharePoint site? The network device running-configuration itself?

Using the new NDLC, a living source of truth in TFS exists. A rich repository containing data models, templates, and Ansible playbooks which also stores the compiled, intent-based, dynamically generated configuration files for each device. TFS is a single, central, RBAC controlled, source of truth for the network. TFS repository can be used as a reference for all future network designs and troubleshooting.

Source of truth means browsing for data models or templates that create the configuration or the compiled output showing the exact device configuration, without ever needing to connect to the device CLI. Other artifacts such as the routing tables or firewall rule lists can also be stored in the source of truth as output from dynamic playbooks. Having this is not something every network can produce; however, it is indispensable when designing new features, planning future changes, dealing with network failures or troubleshooting problems.

Change Management

Network automation can help simplify the change management process as it is a natural part of a pull request. The master branch can be locked, and only approved changes allowed to be merged through a pull request. An approver has all the necessary artifacts to approve, deny, or conditionally reject a pull request asking the developer for more details. Documentation is automatically generated and the changes to either the data model or dynamic template of a device is obvious and highlighted in TFS for the approvers benefit.

Sample Processes:

- New requirement / change / feature / correction / refactoring.
- Added to work board in TFS.
- Work assigned.
- New working branch created.
- Engineer performs **git pull** downloading the updates to the central repository.
- Engineer changes to new branch in local VS Code **(git checkout)**.
- Development work:
  - Add / change / delete code.
  - Testing – check mode.
  - Documentation generated.
- Engineer performs commits often, ideally for small related changes.
- Engineer performs a **git push** uploading the changes to the central repository.
- Engineer submits a pull request in TFS.
- Pull request triggers approval workflow.
- Approvers / reviewers notified.
- Pull request approved or denied.
- Approved request merged into master branch.
- Automated build triggered.
- Documentation updated.
- Automated test triggered.
- Automated release scheduled.
- Change delivered to environment through Ansible.
- Alternatively, if full CI/CD automation is not yet established, operators execute approved Ansible playbooks manually.

Problem Resolution

Being able to quickly identify, troubleshoot, and resolve network problems becomes an easier process with the addition of these new tools. CLI skills are still required but think of automation as an augmentation and extension of the network team's skills, providing results at scale in near real-time. The source of truth can be referenced using pull requests and commit information to find the last changes and how they relate to outages. The automated documentation can be used to confirm configurations and key information about devices without the need to connect to any device. Ansible can also be used to rapidly deploy a fix to the enterprise if a flaw is found or a change to multiple devices is required to resolve an issue. This method has the benefit of being included in the source of truth and master branch for future reference.

Resources

Network staff may not adapt to change as rapidly as other IT disciplines, mainly because the way networks are managed has not changed all that much over the past 30 years. However, network staff should always be looking for the most effective way to manage the network. Most will fully embrace this new methodology because of the power it unlocks and how much easier it will make their lives in the long run. Once the transition has been made resources can be reallocated to more strategic projects. Ultimately, a stronger workforce emerges with modern, diverse problem-solving skills, software development principals and basic coding abilities. There may not be a place for the CLI warrior in the next-generation network.

Cost

Capital expenditure savings can be achieved using network automation. Instead of large, expensive, appliance-based NMS solutions or agent-based software solutions, build an in-house solution custom fit to the organization's needs. Even larger savings can be realized in operational expenditures. Time spent in manual CLI device-to-device configurations or information gathering is eliminated. Overtime incurred for after hour changes is drastically reduced. Changes that took hours now take minutes. Large disruptive changes take significantly less time and effort because the power of the automation engine is orchestrating and delivering the solution. These are huge benefits to any organization and demonstrates an immediate ROI. It is hard to put a price on having a central repository acting as a source of truth for the network.

Provisioning

One capability to consider, now that configuration management is automated, is device provisioning. Provisioning new devices is a repeatable, one-time task and an ideal candidate for automation. Some "zero-touch" provisioning solutions exist as part of NMS solutions however they are often complex, and mileage may vary. Using a homegrown automation solution, several options are available to automate provisioning, however, these options still require one or two touches to the device.

An operator can generate an automated configuration using data models, dynamic templates, and the Ansible framework. Then they transfer the generated golden configuration to a USB drive and connect to the console replacing the start-up configuration of the device with the generated, templated, configuration.

Alternatively, the operator can use the console to configure the device with bare minimum requirements to be delivered in place. Connect the device to the network and push the generated configuration over SSH using an Ansible playbook. The device requires some initial configuration for reachability including a management IP address, SSH access over VTY lines, and the appropriate uplink interfaces configured before delivering on-site. Once installed and connected, the remaining golden configuration is put in place using the automation engine.

Either method guarantees that all net-new network devices adhere to the golden configuration with little to no effort from operations. Also, by using the new NDLC, a dedicated working branch represents an exact point-in-time in the master branch of when the device was added to the network.

Peripheral changes made to accommodate the new device, for example, the uplinking device, routing tables, or other changes beyond the newly provisioned device itself, are captured in the working branch. The ability to perform side-by-side historical comparisons from before and after the change is available in the TFS history viewer and along with it being automatically provisioned, the new device also comes with automatically generated documentation.

Source Control

The following is another way of looking at source control, in the context of network as code. If only code from the master branch is deployed to the network, the state of the network at any given point-in-time is known. If there are no out of band changes, the entire history and evolution of the network is captured in the master branch history. Controlling this source code is extremely important given the blast radius a problem on the network can have. Locking the master branch, forcing working branches for all changes, implementing strong RBAC, and utilizing pull requests that require outside approvals, are all forms of source control TFS offers.

Version Control

Automated builds give a sense as to the "version" of the network code and device configurations. Using pull requests in TFS, changes from the working branch are merged into the master branch. This can trigger an automated build which captures the network's state. Data models, templates, playbooks, tasks, documentation and Git commit history are all included as artifacts in a build. Build numbers increment as the network undergoes changes and vice versa. Begin looking at the network like software:

- Initial build 1.0.
- Add feature – Netflow on distribution layer, all buildings.
- Fix bugs – logic, bad data.
- Build 2.0 – Includes Netflow and fixes x,y,z.

Branching

A Git branching strategy should be adopted and it should be kept simple. Make sure to create working branches for all changes. Also known as feature branches or bug-fix branches, working branches should be limited in scope containing a single change or feature. Within each working branch, use Git to commit changes frequently into the working branch. This allows for distributed development and multiple people to work on the same branch. Keep a high quality golden configuration as the master branch. Use pull requests to merge working branches into the master branch.

A Git branching guide is available here:

https://docs.microsoft.com/en-us/azure/devops/repos/git/git-branching-guidance?view=vsts

To learn more about Git branching, "Learn Git Branching" is a free online interactive training program available here:

https://learngitbranching.js.org/

Summary

The solution to many of the challenges faced by the modern enterprise is network automation. Networks have outgrown the original scale intended for the management plane. Enterprise networks are now made up of hundreds, possibly thousands, of physical and virtual devices and can no longer be managed by larger groups of human operators. The resources required simply cannot keep pace with the demands of new technologies being deployed.

Adopting network automation is an inevitability. The question is whether the technology is available, mature, stable, and production ready for the enterprise. As outlined in Chapter 3, "How to Automate the Network", the tools are available, easy to adopt, and come with mature, well defined, processes.

Chapter 3 How to Automate the Network?

"Change can be frightening, and the temptation is often to resist it. But change almost always provides opportunities - to learn new things, to rethink tired processes, and to improve the way we work."
- Klaus Schwab

How to Prepare the Network?

Network connectivity is obviously a key element of the solution. Network engineers, server administrators, the IT security team, and network operations need to collaborate and determine the architecture for the network automation ecosystem. Communication dependencies between the network devices, the Linux environment hosting Ansible, VS Code, and TFS exist. This guide is designed to help prepare any possible firewall rules or traffic flows that are required depending how the network is zoned. Often servers or workstations that can reach network device management consoles are in a different or highly restricted zone on the network, separated from the operational zone devices like servers or workstations. If using a jump box methodology (connecting from operational zone workstations to management workstations where administrative toolkits are hosted) create standardized all-in-one Windows or Linux hosts with VS Code and Ansible installed. These hosts require communication to TFS and the management console of the network fleet.

It is recommended using device hostnames in the Ansible **hosts.ini** file which allows Domain Name System (DNS) resolution from the Linux environment to lookup the IP address of the network device it is trying to reach. Use hostnames where possible instead of IP addresses in the **hosts.ini** file. Either populate the DNS server the Ansible host is using with the DNS records of the network devices, or statically update the local **hosts** file in the Linux box itself. Again, DNS is recommended over a static Linux hosts file or using IP addresses in the Ansible **hosts.ini** file.

Here are the communication flows required for network automation:

Source	Port	Destination
Ansible	SSH (22)	Network Devices
Git	WebDev / SWebDev (8080 / 8443)	TFS

The network devices do not need to communicate with TFS and Git does not need to communicate to the network devices. Place tools into the appropriate zones or open the appropriate firewall rules to permit these communications.

What Tools are Required?

Microsoft TFS

The Windows administration team needs to setup a TFS environment if one does not already exist. They will establish the architecture for TFS and follow the installation instructions:

https://docs.microsoft.com/en-us/tfs/server/install/get-started/

TFS supports either distributed or stand-alone deployments. After installation, secure TFS with a signed certificate to offer Hyper-Text Transfer Protocol Secure (HTTPS) and Secure Sockets Layer (SSL) services. Active Directory username and passwords can be required to allow Git interactions with TFS, primarily for **git clone**, **git pull**, and **git push** operations, or keys can be exchanged between the Ansible host and TFS. Once TFS is installed and available, determine the TFS administrators and assigned Role-Based Access Controls (RBAC). Create the base repositories for the environments (lab, production) along with the master branch in each repository. Git is natively supported in TFS so select Git at the repository type selection. Assign permissions to the repositories and distribute the TFS workspace hyperlink to the network administrative staff. TFS also acts as a graphical front-end for Git presenting all the important information found in Git, such as commit details, in an easy to use feature-rich ecosystem.

This book is not intended to be a detailed guide in TFS administration or installation. Please refer to the following guide from Microsoft for further instructions:

https://docs.microsoft.com/en-us/tfs/

Git

Git is natively installed on Linux hosts however should be the first application installed on Windows hosts, if developing in VS Code on Windows. This ensures all the future tools installed will integrate. Git commands can be run from the Windows terminal or from within VS Code editor.

Git command reference

Some commonly used Git commands:

```
git clone <repository url>
```

This will clone a repository into a newly created directory.

For details visit:

https://git-scm.com/docs/git-clone/

```
git checkout <working branch>
```

Navigate and work in multiple branches in the same repository by checking out branches. This does not create another copy of the repository locally, it simply changes to a different branch and Git tracks what branch the changes relate to.

For details visit:

https://git-scm.com/docs/git-checkout/

```
git add
```

Stages locally changed files preparing for the next commit.

For details visit:

https://git-scm.com/docs/git-add/

git commit

Commit changes to the active branch. These commits have an ID that can be used to track the change and act like a check point in the change history. Comparisons in TFS can be done in the GUI showing exactly what changes were made as part of each commit. It is important, especially in a distributed environment, to commit small and focused changes often and only include specific, related changes per commit. It is not recommended to accumulate many local changes and bulk commit them into the branch. Committing often allows for multiple people to collaborate on the same branch and Git will track all the distributed changes across the working branch. This is reflected in the branch history as well as part of the pull request later in the pipeline.

For details visit:

https://git-scm.com/docs/git-commit/

git push

Pushes locally committed changes to the remote repository. It requires authentication against TFS. This is the last step in updating the remote repository with committed updates which pushes the commits into the remote branch.

Take note that this updates the working branch and not the master branch. Use a pull request in TFS to merge the working branch into the master branch in TFS. The master branch should have a history of pull requests while the working branch will have a history of commits.

For details visit:

https://git-scm.com/docs/git-push/

git pull

Pulls down any changes from the remote repository syncing the repository with the remote branch. When working in a distributed environment on a shared branch and commits have been performed on another system it is recommended to refresh your local repository often using `git pull`. Development may be performed in a Windows host using VS Code and may need to be synchronized with the Linux host running Ansible. Changes from TFS need to be pulled locally as they are pushed from the remote host. VS Code can be configured to automatically poll TFS and notify developers that updates for their branch are available.

For details visit:

https://git-scm.com/docs/git-pull/

For more information or to download Git visit:

https://git-scm.com/

Visual Studio Code (VS Code)

VS Code is an extremely powerful text editor and much more. Many extensions are available to enhance Ansible, YAML, Jinja2, Python, and Git readability. VS Code is the main workspace for the modern network engineer writing data models, dynamic templates, tasks, and playbooks.

A lot of the actions in VS Code are Git commands but done through GUI actions. Git is used under the covers to clone repositories locally, change to working branches, make commits, push code to the remote repository, and pull updates from the remote branch. VS Code simplifies development eliminating the need to know these commands.

Extensions

There are many extensions available and they should be explored to find ones that best enhance code readability or functionality. For example, there are Excel-like extensions that view .csv files inside VS Code table style with sorting and filtering capabilities.

Click the "**Extensions**" icon and install the following extensions, at a bare minimum:

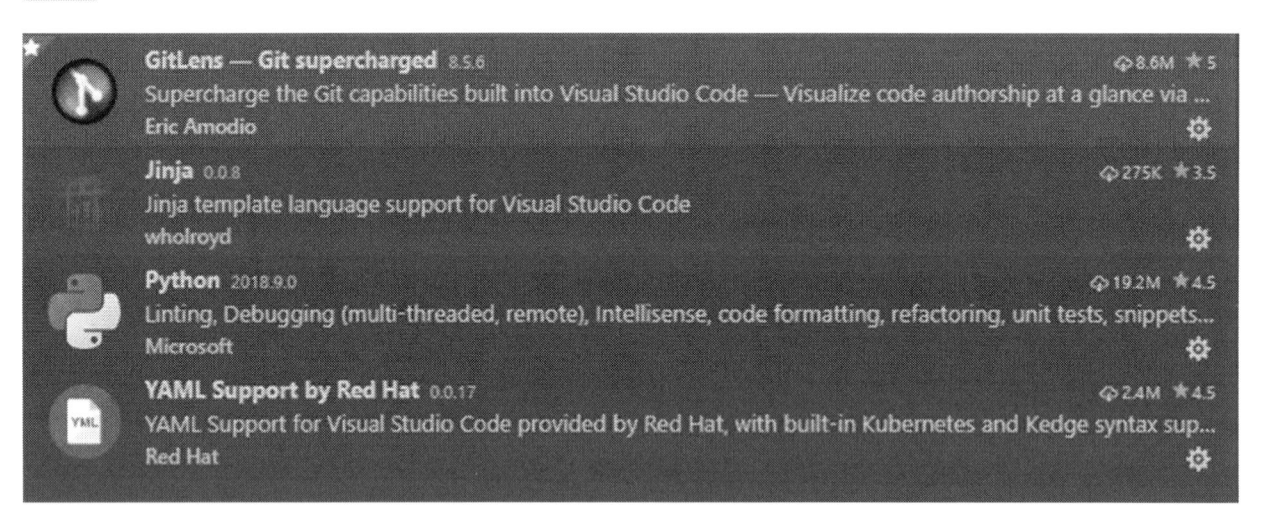

Once Git and VS Code are installed on Windows, repositories can be cloned locally. VS Code has provided a GUI-based overlay to the Git commands.

First, visit *https://github.com/automateyournetwork/Production-Infrastructure/*

Click on "**Clone or download**".

Click the "**clipboard**" to copy the link.

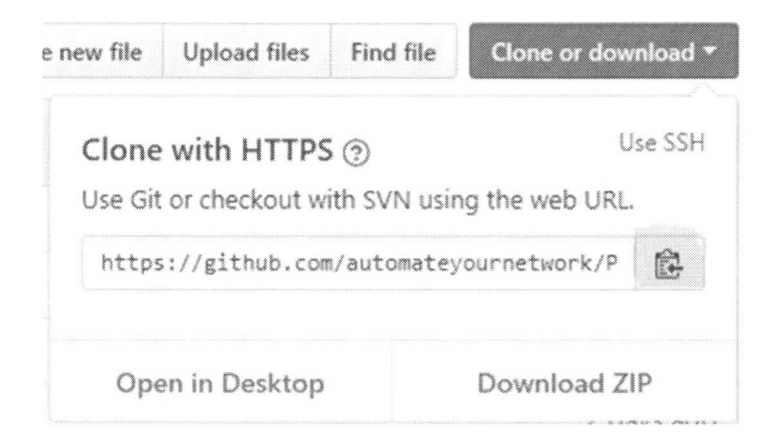

Launch VS Code.

Click the "**gear**" icon in the bottom left corner.

Select "**Command Palette**".

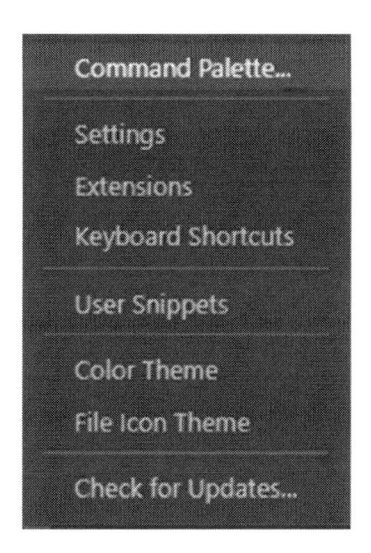

Type in **git clone** and select the command.

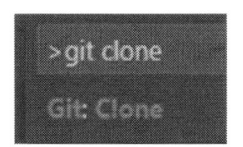

Paste the link into the repository URL.

A Windows dialogue box will appear. Create a folder locally to hold the repository.

Click "**Open Repository**" and open the cloned repository.

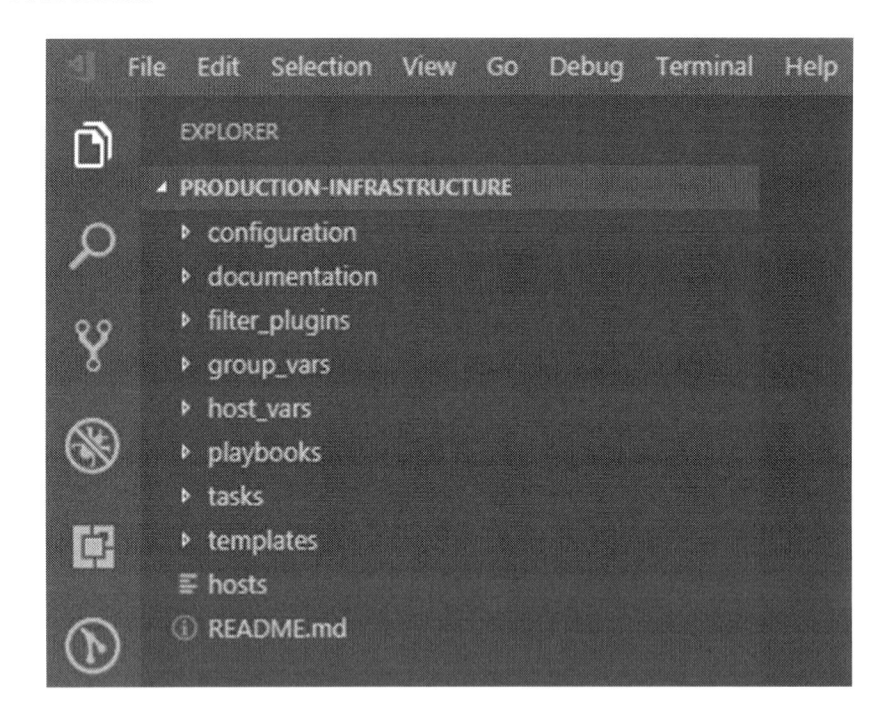

A local copy of the "Automate Your Network Production-Infrastructure" GitHub repository has now been cloned.

VS Code on Linux

VS Code can also run on Linux. For detailed instructions follow this guide:

https://code.visualstudio.com/docs/setup/linux/

It can be advantageous for organizations to build an all-in-one development toolkit host on Linux with VS Code. Code can be developed from within VS Code and Ansible playbooks can be executed from within VS Code directly.

More information about VS Code can be found here:

https://code.visualstudio.com/

Linux

A flavor of Linux is required in the environment to host the Ansible installation. Linux may be new or there might be an existing Linux footprint in the enterprise. The Linux machine where Ansible is installed requires the ability resolve the hostnames, as well as SSH into, all the network devices. The Linux host needs to communicate with the TFS server through TCP port 8080 or 8443 to perform Git operations such as cloning the repository to the Linux host. Using Git, updates from the repository on the TFS server can be pulled down and output from Ansible playbooks can be pushed up into the repository on the TFS server. RBAC should be implemented and standard best practices for server installation (apply updates, harden the system) followed as the Linux host will become a central component of the automation engine. All Ansible playbooks are executed from this Linux host and as such, precautions should be taken to protect this system from unauthorized access.

Traditional Linux

Ansible can run on any Red Hat Enterprise Linux (TM), CentOS, Fedora, Debian, or Ubuntu system.

On Fedora:

```
$ sudo dnf install ansible
```

On RHEL and CentOS:

```
$ sudo yum install ansible
```

On Ubuntu:

```
$ sudo apt-get update
$ sudo apt-get install software-properties-common
$ sudo apt-add-repository --yes --update ppa:ansible/ansible
$ sudo apt-get install ansible
```

A detailed installation guide can be found here:

https://docs.ansible.com/ansible/latest/installation_guide/intro_installation.html

Linux on Windows 10

The Linux requirement should not deter the organization from pursuing Ansible. The enterprise may not support Linux, the network team may not be very familiar with Linux, or it may be a purely Microsoft shop. Linux on Windows is a relatively new supported feature from Microsoft however Ansible has been proven to run under Windows using the latest version of Windows Subsystems for Linux (WSL) and the Ubuntu distribution.

First install WSL. Open the "**Control Panel**".

Click "**Programs**".

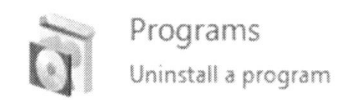

Click on "**Turn Windows features on or off**".

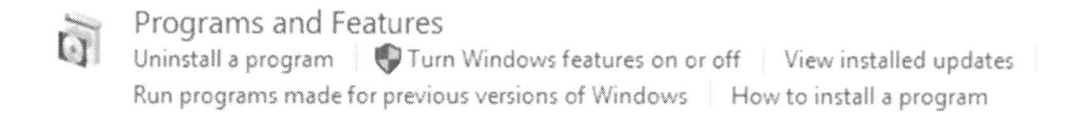

Scroll down and check "**Windows Subsystem for Linux**". Click "**OK**".

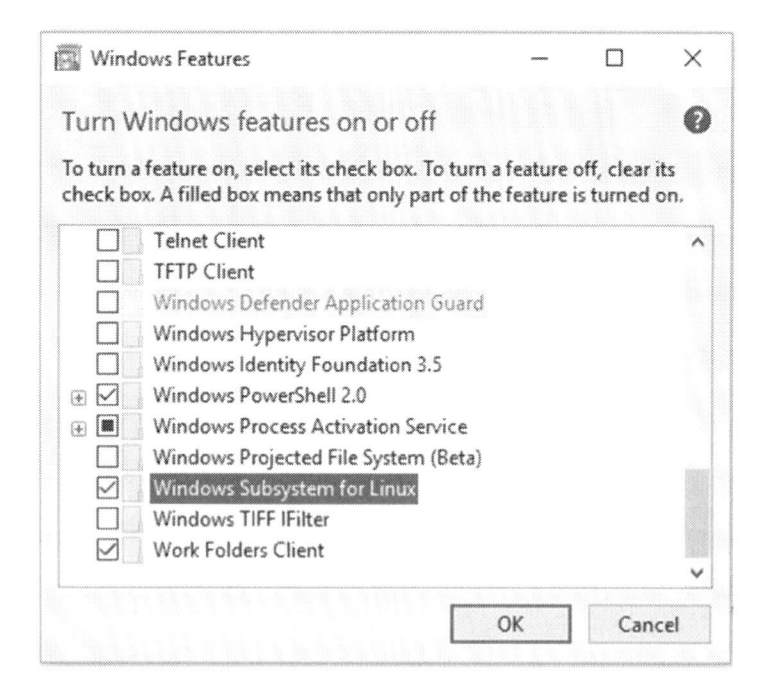

Now install the Ubuntu distribution of Linux on top of Windows.

For example, install Ubuntu from the Microsoft Store.

Microsoft Store
Trusted Microsoft Store app

Ubuntu

Canonical Group Limited • Developer tools > Utilities

⤴ Share

★ ★ ★ ★ ★ 41

Ubuntu on Windows allows one to use Ubuntu Terminal and run Ubuntu command line utilities including bash, ssh, git, apt and many more.

Launch Ubuntu and install Ansible:

```
$ sudo apt-add-repository ppa:ansible/ansible
```

```
$ sudo apt update
```

```
$ sudo apt install ansible
```

Visit *https://github.com/automateyournetwork/Production-Infrastructure/*

Click "**Clone or download**" – click the "**clipboard**" icon.

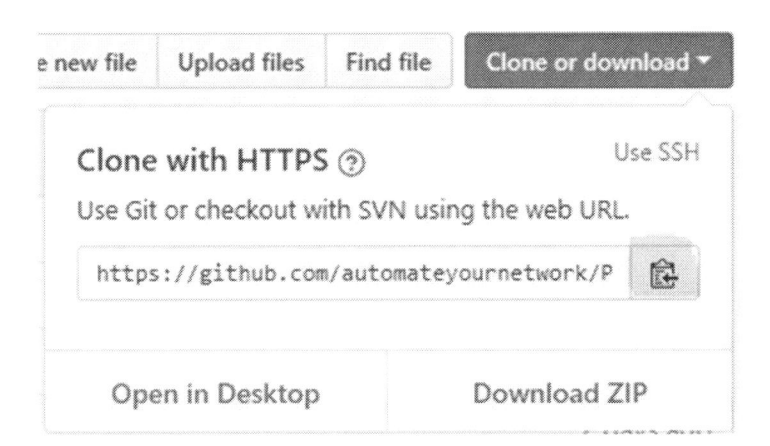

Clone the Automate Your Network repository into the Ubuntu environment.

```
git clone <right-click>
```

Change to the **Production-Infrastructure** folder.

```
automateyournetwork@LINUX HOST:~$ cd Production-Infrastructure
```

Explore the repository.

```
automateyournetwork@LINUX HOST:~/Production-Infrastructure$ ls
```

WSL and DrvFS

Microsoft WSL and DrvFS can be used to set the permissions using traditional Linux **chmod** commands. If errors are encountered when running Ansible playbooks in Windows particularly because the **ansible.cfg** file has world write permissions, use the following instructions to open **chmod** capabilities in Ubuntu:

First unmount the drive.

```
sudo umount /mnt/c
```

Then remount the drive including the meta data.

```
sudo mount -t drvfs C:/mnt/c -o metadata
```

Now set permissions on the repository.

```
chmod -R 755 /home/user/Production-Infrastructures
```

Please refer to the following blog for more details about WSL and DrvFS:

https://blogs.msdn.microsoft.com/commandline/2018/01/12/chmod-chown-wsl-improvements/

Ansible playbooks can now be executed from the Windows 10 machine.

Ansible

Ansible is the automation engine where playbooks are run, either in check mode or full execution mode. Running playbooks is as simple as creating a YAML file and running the **ansible-playbook** command in the Linux host.

The syntax for **ansible-playbook** is as follows:

```
ansible-playbook <playbook file name.yml> <options>
```

Some common options:

--ask-vault-pass	ask for vault password.
-C, --check	do not make changes; instead, try to predict some of the changes that occur.
-D, --diff	when changing (small) files and templates, show the differences in those files; works great with –check.
-l SUBSET, --limit=SUBSET	further limit selected hosts to an additional pattern.

--start-at-task=START_AT_TASK	start the playbook at the task matching this name.
--step	one-step-at-a-time: confirm each task before running.
--syntax-check	perform a syntax check on the playbook, but do not execute.
-t TAGS, --tags=TAGS	only run plays and tasks tagged with these values.
-v, --verbose	verbose mode (-vvv for more).

Scope of Playbook

The scope of what devices to run a playbook against is included in the playbook itself but can be overridden using the – **limit** option. This is useful if the playbook is configured, for example, to run against the entire campus but there are only changes for a single device or subset of devices. Use the – **limit** option and provide a group or hostname from the **hosts.ini** file to specify which devices to run the playbook against at run time.

```
ansible-playbook <playbook.yml> --limit <host / group>
```

Check Mode

Check mode can be used to dry run Ansible playbooks, and as part of the change management process. It is a validation step before pull requests are approved. The output from check mode can be made a mandatory artifact. The results from check mode show exactly what devices will be changed and the exact configuration commands that will be executed and in what order. Check mode is often combined with a level of verbosity to display more details about what the Ansible playbook would have changed, as opposed to simply indicating a change. This data is a gold mine of information that can be used to help the NetDevOps team collaborate and fully understand a change before it is deployed.

```
ansible-playbook <playbook.yml> --check -v
```

Idempotency

Much like check mode, the state of playbook idempotency is another source of non-technical information NetDevOps can leverage. An understanding of how far ahead or behind either the source of truth or the production environment is from each other becomes very clear using check mode capabilities. Once idempotency is achieved, be sure no out of band changes are made (only automated changes using the automation engine and NDLC process) and the branching strategy is followed to maintain the idempotent state.

Modern Development Toolkit

To maximize efficiency, consider building a development toolkit system used for everyday development of Ansible playbooks. Either build a Linux-based system with Microsoft VS Code installed, or a Windows-based system with Linux installed. Either way, have a system that includes:

- A flavor of Linux.

- Ansible.
- Git.
- VS Code.
- Connectivity to TFS through TCP ports 8080 / 8443.
- Connectivity to network devices management IP via SSH (TCP port 22).

Modern Network Development Lifecycle (NDLC)

With new tools comes new processes and procedures. Below is a high-level overview of the modern NDLC using all the tools introduced above. This includes a simple branching strategy. The organization should decide on its own branching strategy, for example, a new branch for every change, no long-lived branches, and no branching beyond two branches. For now, we will adopt a new branch per change approach with one level of branching.

- Create a repository specific to the environment in TFS:
  - Examples include: Production, Lab, Development.

- Create a master branch:
  - The master branch will be what is considered tested, approved, current, golden configurations and code.
  - Never develop or make changes directly inside the master branch.
  - Use Git commits and pull requests to merge changes into the master branch.
  - Playbooks should be executed from the master branch.

- Create a working branch:
  - All changes performed in working branch.
  - Playbook tested and validated possibly with check mode and verbosity.
  - Changes understood.
  - Commits from local repository made often to ensure TFS version updates often.
    - Prevents local work from being lost.
    - Ensures ability to collaborate on branches.
  - Pull request to merge changes into master branch.
    - An entire workflow can be created from the pull request.
    - Various QA and approvals.
    - Changes merged successfully into master branch.

- Clone repository locally:
  - `git clone`
  - Brings the repository down to a local Windows or Linux machine.
  - Extremely portable provided Linux and Ansible are installed.

- Change to working branch:
  - `git checkout`
  - VS Code GUI to change into new working branch.

- Make changes:
  - Modify existing files.
  - Create new files.

- o Delete files.

- Stage changes:
  - o `git add`
  - o VS Code GUI to save local changes.

- Commit changes:
  - o `git commit`
  - o Using VS Code GUI.
  - o Add meaningful comment to the commit.
  - o Commit is referenced and available in TFS and VS Code.

- Push changes:
  - o `git push`
  - o VS Code synchronization.
  - o This finalizes the commit and pushes the files into the central repository.

- Pull request:
  - o A pull request in TFS is created to merge the working branch into the master branch.
  - o A full workflow can accompany this pull request that could require reviewers and approvals.

- Version and change control:
  - o All changes can be referred to by their pull request.
  - o Each pull request comprised of Git commits.
  - o Complete history of changes to all files available through TFS.
  - o Easy roll-backs.
  - o Easy troubleshooting problematic changes.

Microsoft TFS Central Repository Features

Microsoft TFS is much more than a centralized repository for the code. It is a full development ecosystem enabling cross-team collaboration, as well as version and source control. TFS also acts as a GUI for Git and automates software builds, testing and releases.

Work items can be assigned, tracked, and used to create working branches for new code. Work items should have limited scope such as a new feature request, bug-fix, or enhancement to the code.

Welcome

Get started using Team Foundation Server to make the most of your team dashboard.

 Manage Work
Add work to your board

New items can be added by anyone with the correct permissions and can be directly assigned to individuals or left open for developers to take ownership themselves.

Working branches, sometimes called feature branches and bug-fix branches, can and should be created for every work item and change made to the repository (and therefore the network) and changes committed often to these working branches, so developers can collaborate using the CI model.

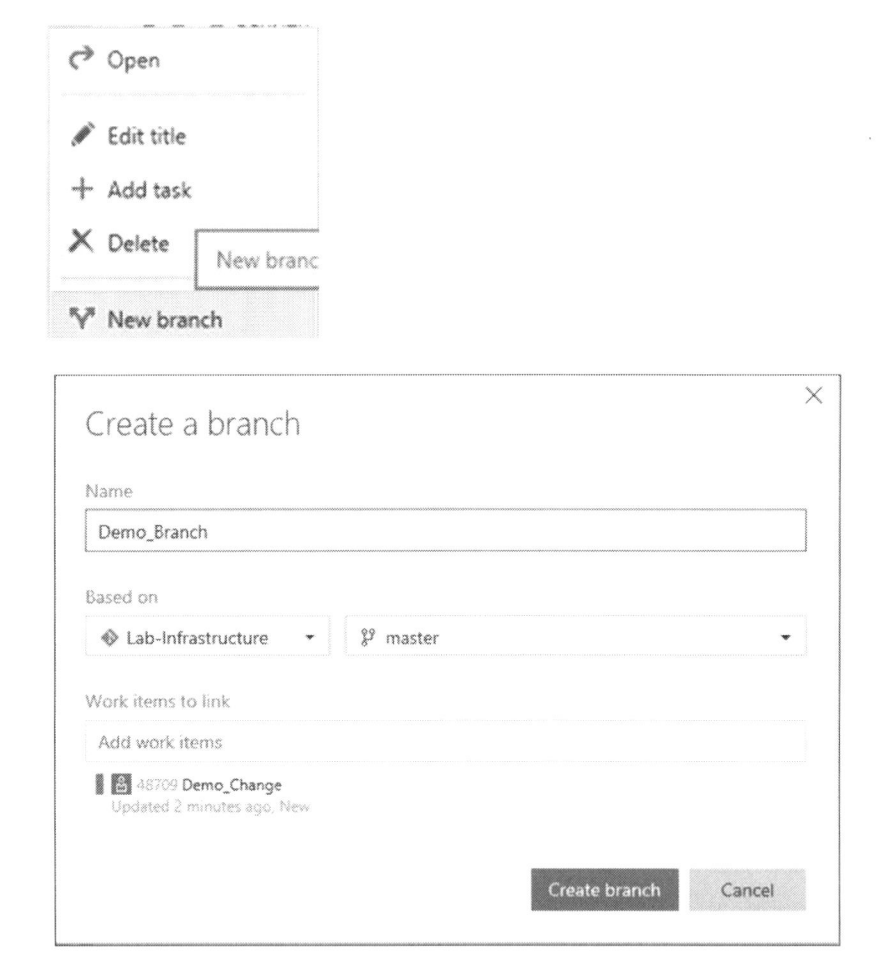

The central repositories can be explored through the browser including the complete history of every element of code, all the current and previous branches, and pull requests, including the related Git commits.

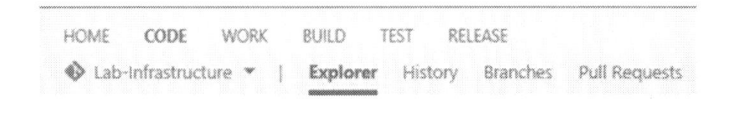

TFS **History** is a rich source of information and an easy way to explore the changes made to the network. Troubleshooting problems becomes infinitely easier now that changes can be viewed in reverse sequence of application. Problems can be pin-pointed to an exact pull request as well as the commit involved in making the change.

Each of these **Branch Updates** can be expanded for a summary of commits into this branch.

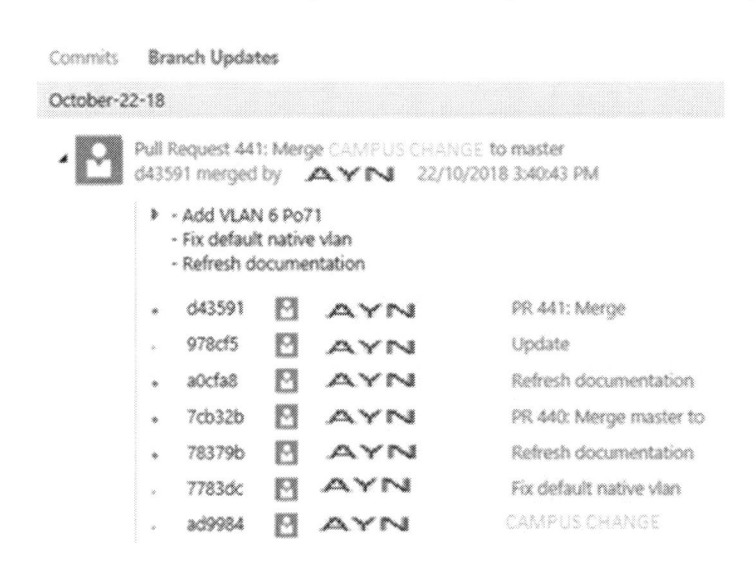

The **Branches** view provides a detailed view of the master branch, all working branches, and their relative state. Branches can be ahead or behind the master branch and the details of what code in which files is different can be determined using the **Branches** view.

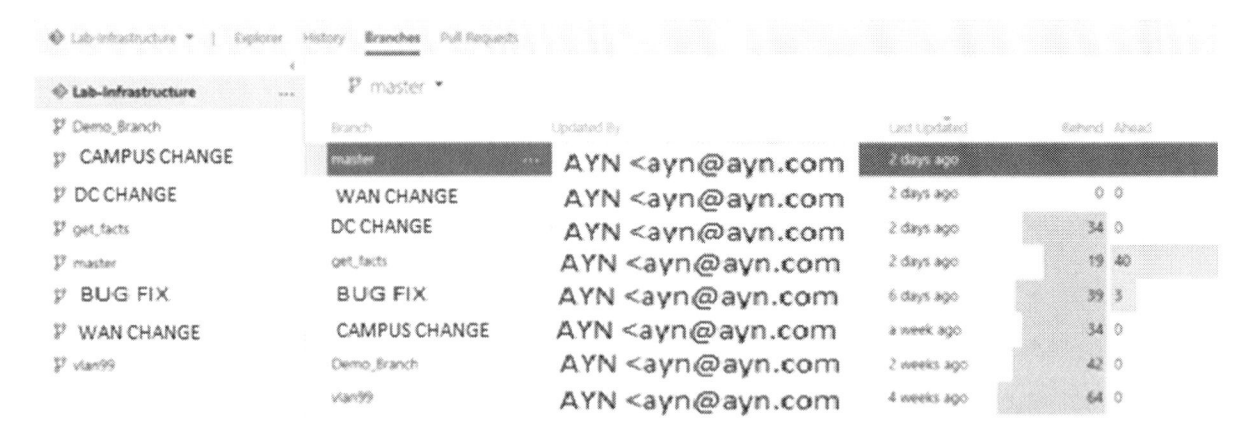

Completed or pending **Pull Requests** along with their commit history can be explored.

Pull Requests can be initiated to:

- Merge a working branch into the master branch.
- Merge a working branch into another working branch.
- Merge the master branch into a working branch, possibly to refresh an older branch or bring a working branch up to parity.

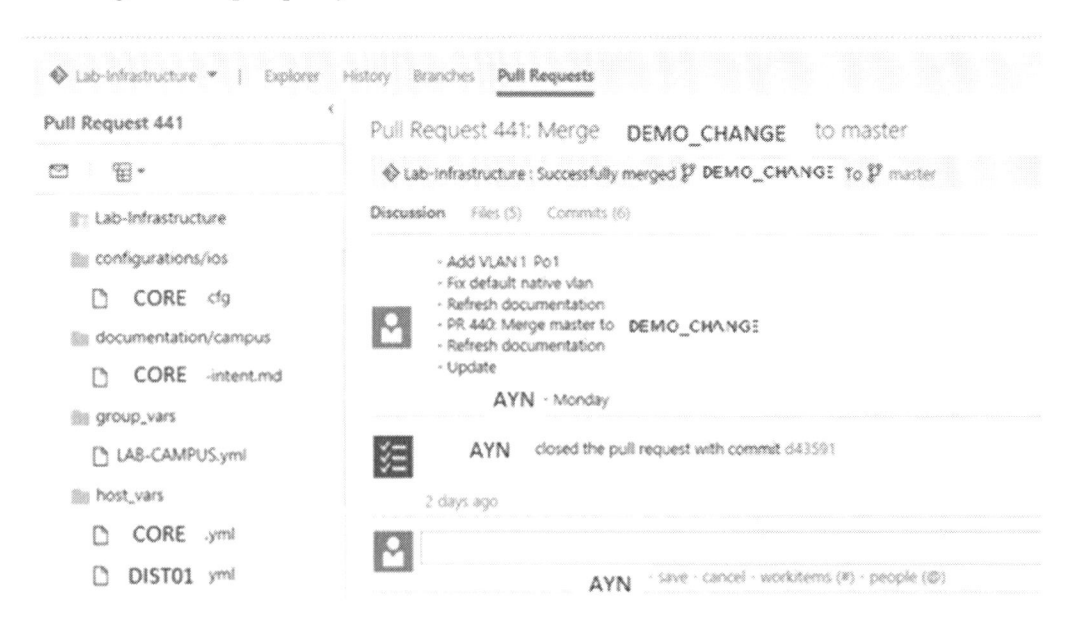

Completed **Pull Requests** can be viewed along with the changes that were merged into the master branch.

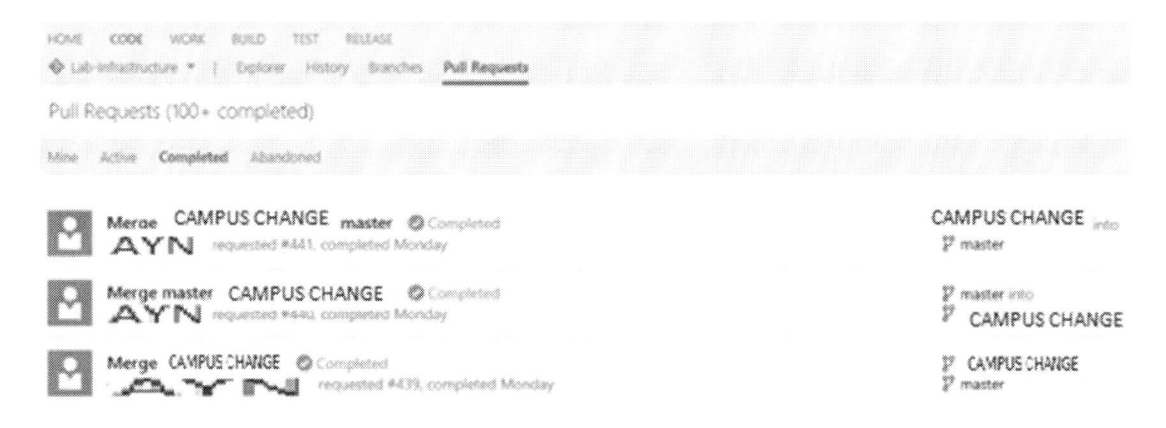

Summary

Network automation is more than just a set of new tools and technologies. It includes adopting a modern network development lifecycle. The network needs to be prepared for the necessary communication flows between the tools and the environment. Several new technologies, including Microsoft Team Foundation Server, Microsoft Visual Studio Code, Git, Linux, and Ansible, need to be installed. Once established, the network automation ecosystem allows you to begin the next steps to complete network automation. Chapter 4 is a guide for the first steps to using the new network automation system.

Chapter 4 Where to Start with Network Automation?

"Start by doing what's necessary; then do what's possible; and suddenly you are doing the impossible."
- Francis of Assisi

There may be immediate needs for an automated solution and while it may be tempting to jump right into making automated changes to the network, it is strongly recommended to begin with information gathering. Spend time breaking down the network into the building blocks of enterprise design and logical functions. For example:

- Enterprise lab network.
  - o Core.
  - o Distribution.
  - o Access.
- Enterprise campus network.
  - o Core.
  - o Distribution.
  - o Access.
- Enterprise data center.
- Enterprise WAN.
- Enterprise DMZ / Public Access Zone (PAZ).
- Public and private clouds.

To select the required Ansible modules, and to identify differences in configuration syntax, further break down the network into hardware platforms and software versions. Code differences exist between platforms for the same commands or configurations. Now that configurations are being automated, with a goal of idempotency, coding for the sometimes-subtle differences in running-configurations across the various platforms and software version in the enterprise is a necessity. The more standardized the platforms across the network, the more uniform the code becomes. Here is an example of a network hardware audit:

- IOS – Catalyst 6500.
- IOS – Catalyst 4500.
- IOS – Catalyst 3850.
- IOS – Catalyst 3750.
- IOS – Catalyst 3560.
- IOS – Catalyst 2960.
- NXOS - Nexus 7K.
- NXOS - Nexus 5K.
- IOS - ISR 881.

Start thinking about various common functions or features enabled on the network. Note any commonalities amongst groups of devices by platform, IOS, or function. This will help identify patterns in the configurations to help in writing templates later. For example:

- Core Layer:
  - o Catalyst 6500 platforms.
  - o Virtual Switching System (VSS).

- o Unique QoS model.
  - o VLANs.
  - o VRFs.
  - o OSPF / EIGRP / Static routing.
  - o Port-channels.
  - o Physical interfaces.
  - o Virtual interfaces.
    - ▪ IP addresses.

- Distribution layer:
  - o Catalyst 4500 platforms.
  - o VSS.
  - o Standardized QoS model (MQC).
  - o ACLs.
  - o VLANs.
  - o VRFs.
  - o OSPF / EIGRP / Static routing.
  - o Physical interfaces.
  - o Virtual interfaces.
    - ▪ IP helpers.
    - ▪ IP addresses.

- Access layer:
  - o Catalyst 3850 platforms.
    - ▪ QoS model same as 4500 (MQC).
    - ▪ Stackwise technology.
    - ▪ Power stacking.
  - o Catalyst 3750 platforms.
    - ▪ Unique QoS model (MLS).
    - ▪ Stackwise technology.
    - ▪ Power stacking.
  - o Catalyst 3560 platforms.
    - ▪ QoS model same as 4500 (MQC).
  - o Catalyst 2960 platforms.
    - ▪ Unique QoS model (MLS).
  - o ACLs.
  - o VLANs.
  - o Physical interfaces.
    - ▪ Various profiles.
    - ▪ Wireless Access Points.
    - ▪ PoE devices.
    - ▪ Spanning-tree protocol settings.
    - ▪ VLAN.
    - ▪ Voice.
    - ▪ QoS.
    - ▪ Security.
  - o Virtual interfaces.
  - o Default gateways.

- IOS and NXOS global configuration enterprise standards:
  - Banners.
  - AAA.
  - RADIUS.
  - NTP.
  - DNS.
  - SNMP.
  - Syslog.
  - Archive.
  - Boot version.
  - Standard global configurations.

As expertise improves, identify other candidates for future automation to expand the scope of coverage. Most devices will follow the same methodology used to automate network devices. Other candidates include:

- Data center networking.
- Load-balancers.
- Firewalls.
- Network appliances / controllers.
- Storage devices.
- Cloud.
- Windows Servers.
- Linux Servers.

A library of supported vendors and available Ansible modules can be found here:

https://docs.ansible.com/ansible/latest/modules/modules_by_category.html

Network Automation Readiness Evaluation

Before beginning to write playbooks or creating data models, take time to evaluate the network for automation readiness. Automating a poorly-designed network is a much more difficult task than automating a well-designed network. In fact, it might not be possible to fully automate a network that lacks basic standards. After all, a big step in network automation is full configuration management that leverages dynamic templates. A network without basic standards cannot be templated. The ability to automatically gather information and run one-time tactical playbooks exists, however full configuration management may be difficult to achieve. Some items to consider when determining network readiness:

- Campus design – core, distribution, access layers.
- Layer 1:
  - Physical connectivity.
  - Standardized interfaces for uplinks.
  - Copper or fiber.
  - Speeds.
- Layer 2 / layer 3:
  - Boundary at the distribution layer.
  - Standard VLANs.
  - IP address scheme.

- - Established patterns for buildings / floors on the campus access.
  - Summarized IP address spaces.
  - Meaningful IP addresses.
  - Some standards for point-to-point links, routes and routing tables.
- Naming conventions.
- Standardized servers for NTP, DHCP, DNS, syslog and SNMP.
- IOS versions.
- QoS models.
- Standard port configurations:
  - SVIs.
  - Physical ports.
  - Port-channels.
  - Access ports.
  - Trunk ports.
- Access port standards:
  - Data and voice VLANs.
  - STP toolkit.
  - QoS.
  - 802.1x.
  - Port description.
  - PoE.
- Trunk port standards:
  - Native VLAN.
  - VLAN list.
  - Port description.

Ironically, the first automated task may be using Ansible to perform the network reconnaissance to prepare the network for Ansible.

At this point, confirm that all the architectural components are in place and are able to communicate with each other. If not, work with the network operations team or server administrators to help finalize the environment. A final checklist:

- Microsoft TFS Server:
  - Configured and licensed.
  - RBAC in place.
  - Repository created for environment.
  - Link to repository published.
  - Able to communicate with VS Code / Git on developers' workstations.
  - Able to communicate with Linux / Git on host running Ansible (if not same host as VS Code development host).
  - Certificates and PKI.

- Linux host:
  - Can reach network devices through SSH.
  - Can reach TFS via 8080 / 8443.
  - Ansible installed.
  - Repository cloned locally from TFS.

- VS Code:
    - Installed on either Windows or Linux developer workstation.
    - Extensions installed for Python, YAML, Jinja2, Git, Ansible, and other file formats.
    - Repository cloned locally from TFS.

- Network:
    - Service account created for Ansible playbooks to authenticate.
    - Ansible playbooks have method of authenticating.

Processes and NDLC

New organizational processes need to be adopted and formalized before beginning, even if only in the information gathering phase. This ensures new processes have time to take hold and the team is ready to follow the new NDLC. This new NDLC includes:

- Creation of a centralized TFS repository.
- Creation of a master branch.
- Using working branches, such as feature requests or bug fixes, for all changes.
- Committing code often using Git.
- Using pull requests to merge tested code into the master branch.
- Establish the associated approval workflow in TFS.

Iron out the details of this process before starting to build the solution. To make the change gradual and the transition smooth, have new automation meetings and discuss possible quick wins or any immediate needs that can be met using the newly available capabilities. Focus on how information gathering, and network reconnaissance playbooks will be of immediate value to network operations. Get the operations team excited and involved in running and requesting playbooks. Build a library of reconnaissance tools gradually moving towards automating changes.

Training and Transition

The transitionary phase is likely one of the most painful parts of adopting any new technology. There is natural resistance to change. Several new tools are being introduced all at once. Stressing the importance of following the new processes for network management is the most important component of a successful transition to network automation. The philosophy of "automate everything" must be adopted by everyone for this to work. Manual out-of-band changes cannot be tolerated once full automated network configuration management has been put into effect. Conflicts between the manual changes and the source of truth will exist. Most likely, these manual changes will be overwritten and lost the next time an automated change is made. This occurs because the changes were never added to the code repository which leaves the network potentially impacted with no way to track what happened. This hazard exists and therefore should be avoided at all costs. Staff need to be educated on the serious and negative consequences of making manual changes.

Network engineers will need a substantial lead ahead of network operations as they will likely be the ones writing the initial playbooks and converting the network to code. Network operations can then be trained on how to execute the playbooks. Over time, more NetDevOps can be adopted and network operations can start updating the data models and potentially write their own information gathering playbooks, while the network engineers continue to write logical templates and potentially more complex, or new, data models.

Build Repository Folder Structure

The first step in building the automation ecosystem is setting up the first TFS repository for the selected environment the organization has decided to automate. The repository is the foundation for the NDLC and the source of truth, so it is very important to create a structure that scales and imposes rigid standards. RBAC should be configured limiting access to the code base as appropriate.

Distribute the link to the network developers once the security and workflows are in place. Create the first branch - the master branch - which includes the base folder structure and inventory **hosts.ini** file. A recommended folder structure is covered in Chapter 5. Lock the master branch once populated.

Create Ansible Inventory File - hosts.ini

Once ready to start populating the repository, begin with the foundational **hosts.ini** file. A considerable amount time should be spent creating a hierarchical model for the **hosts.ini** file, building natural logical groups of devices where applicable. These groups are more than just a list of hosts. The group name itself becomes a key accessible to create a **group_vars** YAML file as a data model for all the hosts listed under a group. Organize the **hosts.ini** file to reflect the logical network topology. Ansible can execute playbooks against different technologies at the same time. For example:

- ```
  [ENTERPRISE:children]
  CAMPUS
  DATA-CENTER
  WAN
  DMZ
  ```

- ```
  [CAMPUS:children]
  CAMPUS-CORE
  CAMPUS-DISTRIBUTION
  CAMPUS ACCESS
  ```

- ```
  [CAMPUS-CORE]
  CORE
  ```

- ```
  [CAMPUS-DISTRIBUTION]
  DIST01
  DIST02
  ```

- ```
  [CAMPUS-ACCESS:children]
  CAMPUS-ACCESS-3850
  CAMPUS-ACCESS-3750
  ```

- ```
  [CAMPUS-ACCESS-3850]
  ACCESS01
  ACCESS02
  ```

- ```
  [CAMPUS-ACCESS-3750]
  ACCESS03
  ```
  ```

- `[DATA-CENTER:children]`
  `LAB-DATA-CENTER-7K`
  `LAB-DATA-CENTER-5K`

- `[DATA-CENTER-7K]`
  `DC01_7K`
  `DC02_7K`

- `[DATA-CENTER-5K]`
  `DC01_5K`
  `DC02_5K`

- `[WAN:children]`
  `WAN-ISR`
  `WAN-ACCESS`

- `[WAN-ISR]`
  `WANISR01`

- `[WAN-ACCESS]`
  `WANACCESS01`

- `[DMZ]`
  `DMZ01`
  `DMZ02`

For more information about working with inventory files in Ansible visit:

https://docs.ansible.com/ansible/latest/user_guide/intro_inventory.html

The Linux host needs to be able to resolve these hostnames. Ideally, populate the DNS server records so Ansible can dynamically resolve the hostnames. Otherwise update the local **/etc/hosts** file and create static records.

Building the **hosts.ini** file might be trivial provided an accurate inventory system, an up to date IP workbook, network topology diagrams or NMS inventory system exists. Otherwise, it may take a bit of manual discovery to ensure complete coverage of the network. At this point the network is operating in manual mode and will be unable to use Ansible to help build its own inventory file. Use Ansible to run the Cisco IOS **show cdp neighbors** commands and use the output to map the network if necessary. Ideally, export a list of devices from your NMS or offline documentation; however, do not underestimate the effort involved in building and maintaining this **host.ini** file.

Gather Information

Network reconnaissance is a massive challenge to tackle on an enterprise network even with powerful network management systems in place. Many commands must be executed at the CLI to capture the information required to troubleshoot a problem or to design a new solution. It can be tedious and cumbersome having to hop from device-to-device and collect information, that could very well be stale or obsolete by the time the change is drafted. It especially does not scale well for larger changes. Now that the inventory file, **hosts.ini**, is ready, Ansible can execute playbooks against the devices. Some advantages to this approach include:

- Excellent starting point to network automation.
- Non-disruptive / non-intrusive / no chance of anything going wrong.
- Simple and easy to get going.
- Basically, converting the commands normally run on a device to a simple script.
- Dry run processes.
- Start building a centralized library of customized network utilities available for engineers or operators to run on-demand or scheduled for execution daily / weekly.
- Start building dynamic network documentation.
- Understand the network:
    o Layer 1 topology.
    o Layer 2 topology.
    o Layer 3 topology.
    o Cisco Discovery Protocol (CDP) neighbors.
    o Open Shortest Path First (OSPF) / Enhanced Interior Gateway Routing Protocol (EIGRP) / Border Gateway Protocol (BGP) neighbors.
    o Routing tables.
    o VLANs.
    o Interface availability / usage.
- Improves software development skills.

Using Ansible offers many ways to gather information from the network. This book focuses on the Cisco **ios_facts** and **ios_command** modules that are natively included with Ansible installation.

Ansible Module – ios_facts

Ansible has a built-in module – **ios_facts** – that can be used to gather facts from the Cisco IOS devices on the network. Simple to use, the **ios_facts** module is a great place to start. Basic information about the hardware, configuration, and interfaces is returned from **ios_facts**. The default setting includes all available facts about a device however it is possible to limit the scope of what **ios_facts** includes or excludes from the playbook. Examples of **ios_facts** usage are included in Chapter 6. It should be noted that other similar fact gathering modules exist such as **nxos_facts**.

A mix of limiting to specific subsets of facts, or every fact but specific subsets, can be used to adjust the scope. Some basic examples from the Ansible **ios_facts** module documentation:

```
# Collect all facts from the device
- ios_facts:
    gather_subset: all

# Collect only the config and default facts
- ios_facts:
    gather_subset:
      - config

# Do not collect hardware facts
- ios_facts:
    gather_subset:
      - "!hardware"
```

For more information about the **ios_facts** module please visit:

https://docs.ansible.com/ansible/latest/modules/ios_facts_module.html

More on Cisco and Ansible:

https://www.ansible.com/integrations/networks/cisco/

Ansible Module – ios_command

Another way of gathering information from the network is using the simple and easy to use **ios_command** module. This module can be used to gather output of IOS **show** commands. Become comfortable with **ios_command**. Build on the ability to gather information from the network and use the module to change the network. Here are some ideas of the **show** commands that can be performed using **ios_command** module to gather network reconnaissance:

- **show cdp neighbors**
- **show spanning-tree**
- **show spanning-tree blockedports**
- **show ip ospf neighbors**
- **show ip route**
- **show ip route vrf**
- **show interface**
- **show interface status**
- **show version**
- **show inventory**
- **show ip interface brief**
- **show arp**
- **show mac-address table**
- **show etherchannel summary**
- **show vlan**
- **show access-list**
- **show policy-map**
- **show tech**

It might seem impossible, however any or all the above commands can be performed on any or all the network devices on demand or at scheduled times using Ansible playbooks. If the output of the commands is kept in the master branch, when changed, TFS will show the change history for these output files. This makes it easier to detect state changes in the network. This could help keep track of topology changes or hint to potential problems or unreported outages. Manipulate the output of the commands and store them in the centralized repository for version and change control.

More on the **ios_command** module can be found here:

https://docs.ansible.com/ansible/latest/modules/ios_command_module.html#ios-command-module

One-Time Ansible Playbooks / Tactical Changes

The automated network reconnaissance has led to some discoveries on the network that need to be addressed such as:

- Large-scale feature deployments.
- Large-scale corrections.
- Single, one-time changes.
- Configuration management.

Ansible Module – ios_config

Building on the **ios_command** module, a new Ansible module - **ios_config** - is used to perform changes on Cisco Catalyst devices running IOS. Think of the **ios_command** module as a tool used in EXEC mode on a device that is able to perform standard **show** commands or **copy running-configuration startup-configuration** commands performed at the user EXEC level of IOS.

In contrast the **ios_config** module can perform privileged EXEC level commands used for device configuration. The **ios_config** module is used to execute commands that make changes on the network.

More on the **ios_config** module can be found here:

https://docs.ansible.com/ansible/latest/modules/ios_config_module.html

Chapter 7 provides examples and expands on **ios_config** utilization to automate tactical one-time plays.

Configuration Management

Ultimately the goal of network automation is to provide complete coverage of all network configurations and required changes to those configurations. One-time tactical playbooks are incredibly powerful however, these playbooks are simply moving the execution of CLI commands from human input to an automation engine. While network reconnaissance and executing tactical commands can be performed at scale, full network configuration management has not yet been achieved because no source of truth exists. The network is not yet intent-based since there is no automated provisioning. The powerful dynamic templating engine has not been put into use.

Automated documentation and configuration management involves the abstraction of data from network configurations. Data models are built around the relevant information a device contains. The actual configuration commands are then transformed into templates. Variables are substituted with information contained in the data models at run time making the templates dynamic. Standardized golden templates ensure configuration consistency derived from intent is applied at scale.

Expand on the utilization of the **ios_config** module to automate network configuration management. For the most part code will continue to be written as YAML files, but now Jinja2 templating is introduced to hold the mix of programmatic logic and static commands to build new templates.

The process can be done in any order but here are the building blocks needed to automate network configuration management:

- Create variables in data dictionary:
    - **group_vars**.
    - **host_vars**.

- YAML file format.
- Abstraction of data from device configuration.
- Key-pair values.
- Lists.

- Create small templates that generate configurations:
  - Jinja2 file format.
  - Dynamic templates.
  - Mix of static text, variables and programmatic logic.
  - Variables replaced with information from **group_vars** and **host_vars**.
  - "For" loops to iterate over lists.
  - Basic "if", "else", and "end if" comparative Boolean logic.

- Create tasks:
  - YAML file format.
  - Cisco **ios_command** module.
  - Call the templates.
  - Assemble the templates.

- Create playbooks:
  - Identify scope. Which devices to execute tasks.
  - Call the tasks.
  - Execute using **ansible-playbook** command and options.

Data Model Structure

Like the investment and thought that went into the **hosts.ini** structure, a lot of up-front time and planning is required to build data model structures. Some basic formatting standards, variable naming conventions and a variable dictionary hierarchy should be established and followed rigidly.

group_vars

As part of the repository structure there is a folder called **group_vars**, which is an Ansible specific folder used to setup data models for the groups configured in the **hosts.ini** file. Group variables are applied to all common hardware platforms or logical functions. If, for example, a common QoS policy is configured on all the distribution switches, abstract the QoS policy data into a model in the **CAMPUS-DISTRIBUTION.yml group_vars** file.

[CAMPUS-DISTRIBUTION] can be called as a **group_vars** by creating a YAML file called **CAMPUS-DISTRIBUTION.YML** inside the **group_vars** folder. This allows the data model to contain variables that apply to all devices listed in **hosts.ini** file subsections creating a golden configuration by platform or logical function.

It is a recommended practice to prepend all variables created in **group_vars** with a common identifier such as **platform_**, **group_**, or **global_**. For example, **platform_defaults** or **group_vlans**. Using this naming convention when writing dynamic templates allows for the intent to become obvious to the operator. It also points to a file in the **group_vars** folder as the source of the data and variable.

The data belonging in **group_vars** or **host_vars** should be considered carefully. There are advantages and disadvantages to either approach. Generally, **group_vars** should contain as many platform or logical function standards as possible and can be used to reflect a solid network design adhering to best practices. Sometimes using **group_vars** does not make sense such as the case of a hostname or management IP address which naturally fits as **host_vars**. Include host information inside the **group_vars** where it makes sense. For example, as a standard, all distribution layer switches should have port-channel 1 configured as the uplink port to the core. Port-channels are usually included as a host variable but in this case port-channel 1 will be listed under the **CAMPUS-DISTRIBUTION.yml** group variable. Some examples of **group_vars** candidates:

- Standard NTP, IP helper addresses for DHCP, SNMP, or syslog servers.
- Access-control lists at the distribution layer.
- QoS policies either by platform, logical function or both.
- Banners.
- AAA configurations such as RADIUS or TACACS+ servers.
- Universal secret.
- Standard interfaces:
  - VSS configurations for core and distribution.
  - Standardized uplinks.
- Domain name.
- Native VLAN.
- Multicast.
- Netflow.
- Platform type identifier.
- Other features with common code across a platform.

host_vars

Similar to **group_vars**, there is a folder in the repository called **host_vars**. In this folder there is a YAML file per device. **DIST01.YML** is the **host_vars** file for that specific network host. Store information that is specific and unique to the device on the network in the **host_vars** YAML files. Depending on the size of the fleet, it may take time to build complete coverage of the devices or configurations. Over time it becomes a matter of cloning an existing **host_vars** YAML file and replacing the data unique to the device.

It is recommended to prepend **host_vars** variables with **hosts_** for ease of readability and reference point as to where the variable is in the repository (in a **host_vars** file). Some examples of **host_vars** variables include:

- Hostname.
- Management SVI IP address.
- VLANs.
- VRFs.
- Routing instances.
- Switch Virtual Interfaces (SVI).
- Physical interfaces.
- Spanning-tree priorities.
- Unique secrets or passwords.

- DHCP servers.
- Switch stack configurations.
- Power stack configurations.

Starting Small

The approach taken to network configuration management may very well determine its success. Do not try to solve everything at once. Break the network down into small modular templates that can easily be read, understood and updated by others. The templates should cover specific functions and features. These small templates can and will be assembled later at run time so do not be afraid to make very small very specific templates as opposed to large one size fits all templates. Use check mode extensively, refactor code, start making manual updates and corrections to the network. Try to achieve idempotency.

Coverage by Configuration

Prior to building templates, create and name empty files in the approximate order the templated configurations are to be executed. It might not be possible to mirror exactly top to bottom configurations of a network device but that is not the goal. The goal is to ensure all the configurations match and will execute in a functional order. The exact line-by-line configurations do not need to match sequentially.

The number of templates created largely depends on the number of technologies and features deployed to the network. There are, however, some common configurations to every network. Here is an example library of small, modular, templates that can be used for a standard campus network. Use this structure to start a dynamic template library. The entire repository is available for cloning, using Git, locally to examine the logic in each template. Remember if **platform_** or **group_** prepends a variable it is stored in a **group_vars** YAML file and applies to a group of devices. If **host_** prepends the variable it is stored in a **host_vars** YAML file. The templates are enumerated to control the serial order of operation in which they are processed.

- 01_IOS_global.j2:
    - Contains device global configuration commands.
    - Static explicit text.
    - Logical operators.
    - Sample:
      ```
      service password-encryption
      service compress-config
      hostname {{ host_defaults.hostname }}
      ```

- 02_IOS_dhcp_server.j2:
    - Devices that act as DHCP servers.

- 03_IOS_management_source.j2:
    - Standardizes management traffic sources.
    - Applied across enterprise.
    - Sample:
      ```
      {% if platform_defaults.type == CORE %}
      ip radius source-interface Loopback0
      logging source-interface Loopback0
      snmp-server trap-source Loopback0
      ```

```
snmp-server source-interface informs Loopback0
ntp source Loopback0
ntp server 192.168.100.100
ntp server 192.168.100.101 prefer
ip ssh source-interface Loopback0
ip tftp source-interface Loopback0
{% else %}
ip radius source-interface Vlan2
logging source-interface Vlan2
snmp-server trap-source Vlan2
snmp-server source-interface informs Vlan2
ip ssh source-interface Vlan2
ip tftp source-interface Vlan2
ntp source Vlan2
ntp server 172.16.0.1 prefer
{% endif %}
```

- 04_IOS_vsl.j2:
    - Virtual switch link configurations for VSS devices.
    - Applied at campus core and distribution layers.

- 05_IOS_powerstack.j2:
    - Switch stack power configurations.
    - Applied at campus access layer.

- 06_IOS_archive.j2:
    - Switch archive configurations.
    - Applied across enterprise.

- 07_IOS_default_gateway.j2:
    - Standardizes the default gateway at the access layer.
    - Requires IP Address scheme with a per-building, per-floor approach.
    - Requries **host_defaults.site** variable in each **host_vars** YAML data model.
    - Sample:

      ```
      {% if platform_defaults.type == 3750 or platform_defaults.type == 3850 %}
      ip default-gateway 172.16.{{ host_defaults.site }}.254
      {% endif %}
      ```

- 08_IOS_energywise.j2:
    - Energy wise configurations.
    - Applied across enterprise.

- 09_IOS_snmp.j2:
    - SNMP related configurations per-device.
    - Applied across enterprise.

- 10_IOS_acls.j2:
    - Access control lists by platform function.
    - Applied globally or uniquely.

- 11_IOS_mls_qos.j2:

- QoS model for legacy multi-layer switching (MLS) QoS.
- Applied at access layer on 3750 platform.

- 12_IOS_6k_qos.j2:
  - QoS model specific to the core or Catalyst 6000 platform.

- 13_IOS_mqc_qos.j2:
  - Modern modular QoS CLI (MQC) model.
  - Applied at both distribution layer on Catalyst 4500 platform and access layer on Catalyst 3850 platform.

- 14_IOS_prefix_list.j2:
  - Standard prefix list commands.
  - Used on core or distribution layers.

- 15_IOS_route_maps.j2:
  - Route maps commands.
  - Applied at core or distribution layers.

- 16_IOS_aaa_rsa.j2:
  - Authentication, authorization, auditing.
  - RSA authentication.
  - Applied across the enterprise.

- 17_IOS_dot1x.j2:
  - 802.1x related configurations.
  - Applied at the access layer.

- 18_IOS_dot1x_radius.j2:
  - 802.1x RADIUS server configurations.
  - Applied at the access layer.

- 19_IOS_vrfs.j2:
  - Virtual Route Forwarding (VRF) related configurations.
  - Applied at the core and distribution layers.
  - Sample:

```
{% if platform_defaults.type == CORE or platform_defaults.type == DIST %}
{%     for host_vrf in host_vrfs %}
{%         if host_vrf == "global" %}
{%         else %}
vrf definition {{ host_vrf }}
{%         endif %}
{%         if host_vrf == "global" %}
{%         else %}
 vnet tag {{ host_vrfs[host_vrf].tag }}
   address-family ipv4
   exit-address-family
{%         endif %}
{%         if host_vrfs[host_vrf].multicast is defined %}
ip multicast-routing vrf {{ host_vrf }}
```

```
{%          endif %}
{%       endfor %}
{% endif %}
```

- 20_IOS_vrf_list.j2:
  - o VRF lists for Easy Virtual Networking (EVN).
  - o Applied at the core and distribution layers.

- 21_IOS_ospf.j2:
  - o OSPF related configurations.
  - o Applied at the core and distribution layers.

- 22_IOS_static_routes.j2:
  - o Static route configurations.
  - o Applied at the core.

- 23_IOS_vlan.j2:
  - o VLAN related configuration.
  - o Mix of global (native VLAN) and per-host application across the enterprise.
  - o Sample:

```
vlan {{ global_campus_defaults.native_vlan }}
  name NativeVLAN
```
  - o
```
{%  if host_vlans is defined %}
{%       for host_vlan in host_vlans %}
vlan {{ host_vlan }}
  name {{ host_vlans[host_vlan].name }}
{%       endfor %}
{%  endif %}
```

- 24_IOS_vlan_interface.j2:
  - o SVI related configurations.
  - o Applied on each host across enterprise.

- 25_IOS_platform_port_channel_interfaces.j2:
  - o **group_vars** implied directly in template name.
  - o All port-channels common to a platform.

- 26_IOS_hostport_channel_interfaces.j2:
  - o **host_vars** implied directly in template name.
  - o All port-channel configurations for an individual device.

- 27_IOS_loopback_interfaces.j2:
  - o All loopback interfaces.
  - o Applied to the core but can be used at distribution or access for management.

- 28_IOS_platform_interfaces_DAD.j2:
  - o Dual Active Detection (DAD) interfaces for VSS systems.
  - o Applied at the core and distribution layers.

- 29_IOS_host_interfaces unused.j2:

- Standard interface configuration for shutdown / unused interfaces.
  - Security controls.
  - Applied on all hosts.
  - A port-profile.

- 30_IOS_host_interfaces_OPZone.j2:
  - Operational zone interfaces.
  - Standard access port configuration.
  - A port-profile.

- 31_IOS_host_interfaces_SECURITY.j2:
  - Interfaces used by security equipment.
  - Locked down access port.
  - A port-profile.

- 32_IOS_host_interfaces_WAP.j2:
  - Configuration for an interface with a wireless access point connected.
  - Some security measures applied along with PoE.
  - A port-profile.

- 33_IOS_host_interfaces_custom.j2:
  - Custom access ports.
  - Do not fit a standard port-profile.
  - Granular control with all interface options available as flags that can be enabled.

- 34_IOS_multicast.j2:
  - Multicast related configurations.
  - Deployed at the core and distribution layers.

- 35_IOS_netflow.j2:
  - Netflow related configurations.
  - Applied at the core, distribution, and access layers.

The templates above, when combined with the information from data models, creates a complete network configuration for a device. Other features that arise can be cloned and be modified versions of existing, working, proven, logic.

Coverage by Platform

Once configurations and features are covered, confirm there are no syntax issues across different IOS platforms. These might be simple spacing differences; however, the templates need to match the running-configuration, or it will never be idempotent. Using check mode with verbosity and checking for idempotency between the coded solution and the running-configurations gives a sense of when coverage has been achieved.

A **documentation.yml** Ansible playbook is developed in Chapter 9. This playbook generates offline copies of the compiled output per-device used to validate syntax, spacing, and used as a source of truth about the intent-based network.

Start evaluating how much of a platform configuration base is covered by the initial 35 templates. If there are gaps or outstanding configurations that remain on the platform and are not covered by a template, write additional templates to cover as much, if not all, of the device's configuration as possible.

Coverage by Logical Function

Like the platform review, ensure the logical layers of the network have adequate coverage using **group_vars**, **host_vars**, and dynamic templates. Confirm that the core, distribution, access, WAN, data center, and DMZ are covered as logical functions when automating the network.

Summary

Getting started can be a daunting undertaking. By breaking down the necessary steps into smaller more manageable components the path leading to network automation can be achievable with very few obstacles. Start with a thorough network readiness assessment, where any gaps can be identified and addressed before beginning. A comprehensive, well-designed, hierarchical inventory file, in the form of **hosts.ini**, ensures coverage of the network. This offers scalability, modularity, and flexibility when executing playbooks. Starting with safe and simple information gathering and network reconnaissance, the organization can start automating network documentation without the possibility of disruption. After gaining confidence and skill the organization can move onto automating tactical changes and task orchestration. Once the network has been standardized and brought into compliance with intent, the network configurations can be abstracted into data models and dynamic templates moving towards full network configuration automation. Finally, a continuous integration and continuous delivery (CI/CD) pipeline is developed achieving full network automation. Concrete examples of this evolutionary journey are found in Part II.

Chapter 4 Where to Start with Network Automation? | 79

Part II

"He's more machine than man now. Twisted and evil."
- Obi-Wan Kenobi

Part II of this book is designed as a practical step-by-step guide that can be followed to automate a network. First configure and understand the base repository file and folder structure. Invest time creating a foundation and folder structure that is logically organized and scalable based on the examples provided in Chapter 5. Once the repository is ready, network reconnaissance can be performed following the examples provided in Chapter 6. Begin using the real-world examples of tactical plays that can be used to make changes to the network starting in Chapter 7. Following the tactical changes, Chapter 8 illustrates how to create data models and dynamic templates. These artifacts are used to further evolve into a fully automated network documentation system in Chapter 9. Chapter 10 uses the data models and dynamic templates to provide a fully automated configuration management system. Chapter 11 explains the CI/CD pipeline to wrap things up.

Remember to Git clone a copy of the supplemental repository to see many more examples of templates:

https://github.com/automateyournetwork/Production-Infrastructure/

Chapter 5 Repository Structure

"The organization of information actually creates new information."
- Richard Saul Wurman

Organization of the repository includes a combination of necessary Ansible framework files and folders as well as user defined files and folders. Create a repository that scales, is easily navigated, and supports the Ansible framework. This should be the first step after creating the environment specific repository in Microsoft TFS. Build the folder structure that best reflects the environment being automated.

Go to TFS.

Create a new "**Work Item**".

Name it initial_repo_config.

Move it to "**Active**".

Clone the repository locally onto the development workstation with VS Code installed.

```
git clone <TFS repository link>
```

Build the structure using empty folders and empty placeholder files that suit the environment. Build a repository suitable for an enterprise campus environment comprised of Cisco Catalyst devices running IOS, and an enterprise data center consisting of Cisco Nexus devices running NX-OS. Remember there are many Ansible modules available from other vendors if not running a Cisco network.

* Important note *: Git will not track or provide version control for empty folders. When creating each folder in the repository create an empty file called **.gitignore**. This ensures the folder structure ends up in the repository. If this file is not created and the folder is left empty the folder will not end up in the repository until a file is present. Once files are added to these folders the **.gitignore** file can be deleted.

More information regarding **.gitignore** can be found here:

https://git-scm.com/docs/gitignore/

Create the base folder structure, **hosts.ini** and a **README.md** file.

```
configuration
documentation
filter_plugins
group_vars
host_vars
playbooks
tasks
templates
hosts.ini
README.md
```

Commit these changes with a meaningful message such as "**Initial folder structure**".

Perform the first pull request and merge the folder structure and completed **hosts.ini** file into the master branch. Delete the working branch **initial_repo_config**.

Test any organizational processes, change controls, approvals, that have been put in place for network automation. Share the link and encourage others to clone the repository.

Move work item to "**Completed**".

Configuration

The configuration folder should have subfolders by platform or operating system to scale and should hold more than just one type of configuration file. The configuration folder holds dynamically generated output that is the result of the **documentation.yml** playbook that will be written later in this book. Think of these files as intent-driven sources of truth and the result of the data models and templates being compiled. Using a folder to hold these files means having an offline version of the configurations that can be referenced. It also means having automated documentation that is updated after every change. It is another way to validate the commands syntax before pushing commands to a device.

```
configuration
|
---- ios
    |
    ---- ACCESS01.cfg
    ---- ACCESS02.cfg
    ---- ACCESS03.cfg
    ---- DIST01.cfg
    ---- DIST02.cfg
    ---- CORE.cfg
---- nxos
    |
    ---- DC01_7K.cfg
    ---- DC02_7K.cfg
    ---- DC01_5K.cfg
    ---- DC02_5K.cfg
---- big_ip
```

Documentation

This is another folder that contains all dynamic documentation files. These can be Markdown (.md) files, excel files (.csv), text files (.txt) or other documentation generated by the playbooks. It is important to remember that since all these files are part of the repository, they all have the same version controls, Git and TFS history, and other meta data as the other files in the repository.

This history can be used to view human-readable output in a Markdown or Excel format instead of trying to read the configuration centric view in the dynamic configuration files in the previous folder.

```
documentation
|
 ---- ios
     |
     ----MD
        |
        ---- ACCESS01.md
        ---- ACCESS02.md
        ---- ACCESS03.md
        ---- DIST01.md
        ---- DIST02.md
        ---- CORE.md
     ----Excel
        |
        ---- ACCESS01.csv
        ---- ACCESS02.csv
        ---- ACCESS03.csv
        ---- DIST01.csv
        ---- DIST02.csv
        ---- CORE.csv
     ----Tactical_Playbooks
        |
        ---- (Output from tactical plays)
     ----Recon_Playbooks
        |
        --- ACCESS01_cdp_neighbors.txt
        --- ACCESS01_running_config.txt
        --- ACCESS01_ios_facts_output.JSON
        --- ACCESS02_cdp_neighbors.txt
        --- ACCESS02_running_config.txt
        --- ACCESS02_ios_facts_output.JSON
        --- ACCESS03_cdp_neighbors.txt
        --- ACCESS03_running_config.txt
        --- ACCESS03_ios_facts_output.JSON
        --- DIST01_cdp_neighbors.txt
        --- DIST01_running_config.txt
        --- DIST01_ios_facts_output.JSON
        --- DIST02_cdp_neighbors.txt
        --- DIST02_running_config.txt
        --- DIST02_ios_facts_output.JSON
        --- CORE_cdp_neighbors.txt
        --- CORE_running_config.txt
        --- CORE_ios_facts_output.JSON
 ---- nxos
     |
     ----MD
        |
        ---- DC01_7K.md
        ---- DC02_7K.md
        ---- DC01_5K.md
        ---- DC02_5K.md
     ----Excel
        |
        ---- DC01_7K.csv
        ---- DC02_7K.csv
        ---- DC01_5K.csv
        ---- DC02_5K.csv
```

```
----Tactical_Playbooks
        |
       ---- (Output from tactical plays)
----Recon_Playbooks
        |
       ---- (Output from recon plays)
---- big_ip
```

filter_plugins

The **filter_plugins** folder is part of the Ansible framework and is a place to store Ansible plug-ins. Ansible plug-ins include Python files that enhance the default capabilities and augment Ansible's core functionality. Write custom plug-ins in Python and store them here.

A complete guide to Ansible plug-ins is available here:

https://docs.ansible.com/ansible/2.7/plugins/plugins.html

group_vars

The **group_vars** folder contains the data models applied to groups of devices found in the **hosts.ini** file. This folder contains YAML files created to contain data models. **group_vars** folder matching the sample **hosts.ini** file are as follows:

```
group_vars
|
 ---- ENTERPRISE.yml|
 ---- CAMPUS.yml
 ---- CAMPUS-CORE.yml
 ---- CAMPUS-DISTRIBUTION.yml
 ---- CAMPUS-ACCESS.yml
 ---- CAMPUS-ACCESS-3850.yml
 ---- CAMPUS-ACCESS-3750.yml
 ---- DATA-CENTER.yml
 ---- DATA-CENTER-7K.yml
 ---- DATA-CENTER-5K.yml
 ---- WAN.yml
 ---- WAN-ISR.yml
 ---- WAN-ACCESS.yml
 ---- DMZ.yml
```

host_vars

The **hosts_vars**, similar to the **group_vars_** folder, contains the data models that apply to each individual device or host in the **hosts.ini** file. This folder again contains YAML files, but in addition a file per-device using the device's hostname is created. **host_vars** folder matching the sample **hosts.ini** file is as follows:

```
hosts_vars
|
 ---- CORE.yml
 ---- DIST01.yml
```

```
---- DIST02.yml
---- ACCESS01.yml
---- ACCESS02.yml
---- ACCESS03.yml
---- DC01_7K.yml
---- DC02_7K.yml
---- DC01_5K.yml
---- DC02_5K.yml
---- WANISR01.yml
---- WANACCESS01.yml
---- DMZ01.yml
---- DMZ02.yml
```

Playbooks

Playbooks is another folder required in the Ansible framework. This is where YAML files that make up Ansible playbooks are stored. It is a good idea to have some structure either by platform or function as well as another level of folders for network reconnaissance playbooks, tactical playbooks, and network management playbooks. Think of these as executables. Use **ansible-playbook** commands to run these playbooks:

```
playbooks
|
---- campus
     |
      ---- tactical
           |
            ---- ospfpoint2point.yml
       ---- recon
           |
            ---- show_cdp_neighbors.yml
            ---- campus_documentation.yml
            ---- ios_command_running_config.yml
        ---- management
           |
            ---- assembled_configure_campus.yml
            ---- configure_campus.yml
 ---- data_center
     |
      ---- tactical
      ---- recon
           |
            ---- show_cdp_neighbors.yml
            ---- dc_documentation.yml
        ---- management
           |
            ---- assembled_configure_dc.yml
            ---- configure_dc.yml
---- WAN
     |
      ---- tactical
           |
            ---- port_channel_fix.yml
       ---- recon
           |
```

```
            ---- show_cdp_neighbors.yml
            ---- wan_documentation.yml
      ---- management
            |
            ---- assembled_configure_wan.yml
            ---- configure_wan.yml
---- DMZ
      |
      ---- tactical
            |
            ---- acl_deployment.yml
      ---- recon
            |
            ---- show_cdp_neighbors.yml
            ---- dmz_documentation.yml
      ---- management
            |
            ---- assembled_configure_dmz.yml
            ---- configure_dmz.yml
```

Tasks

Tasks is another folder required in the Ansible framework. The tasks folder holds all the YAML task files that call Ansible modules. A similar folder structure to the other folders should be created for scalability and to keep tasks sorted by environment and function. The tasks in the configuration's subfolders match one-to-one with each of the Jinja2 template files created. This is not meant to exhaustively cover all the files created but rather to give a picture of the folder structure and samples of the types of tasks required and where to store them:

```
tasks
|
 ---- adhoc
        |
        ---- ios
                |
                ---- copyrunstart.yml
                ---- copyruntftp.yml
        ---- nxos
                |
                ---- copyrunstart.yml
                ---- copyruntftp.yml
        ---- big_ip
 ---- audit
        |
        ---- ios
                |
                ---- ios_gather_facts.yml
                ---- show_ospf_neighbor.yml
                ---- show_ip_route.yml
                ---- show_vrf_details.yml
        ---- nxos
                |
                ---- show_ospf_neighbor.yml
        ---- big_ip
 ---- configurations
```

```
        |
        ---- ios
             |
             ---- assembled_config_campus.yml
             ---- configure_ios_6k-qos.yml
             ---- configure_ios_aaa_rsa.yml
             ---- (a matching .yml file for each Template created)
        ---- nxos
             |
             ---- assembled_config_dc.yml
             ---- configure_nxos_qos.yml
        ---- big_ip
```

The full list of templates is available in the Git repository.

Templates

The templates folder is part of the Ansible framework and is where Jinja2 dynamic template files are kept. Like all the other folders, templates should be structured to scale and organized logically. In the example there are three top level folders: banner, configurations, and documentation. These folders will have subfolders by platform, such as IOS or NXOS. The banner folder is a simple text file that contains the standard banner displayed on all devices when a user logs into the CLI. The configurations folder contains all the dynamic templates used to generate device configurations. The documentation folder contains the templates used to generate the Markdown automated documentation. These templates have a matching YAML file in the tasks folder that includes the module used to compile the commands:

```
templates
|
  ---- banner
       |
       ---- standard_banner.cfg
  ---- configurations
       |
        ---- ios
             |
             ---- 01_IOS_global.j2
             …
             ---- 35_IOS_Netflow.j2
        ---- nxos
             |
             ---- 01_NXOS_global.j2
             …
             ---- 35_NXOS_Netflow.j2
  ---- documentation
       |
        ---- ios
             |
             ---- Access_documentation.j2
             ---- Core_documentation.2
             ---- Distribution_documentation.j2
        ---- nxos
             |
             ---- 7k_documentation.j2
             ---- 5k_documentation.j2
```

hosts.ini

The Ansible **hosts.ini** file needs to be stored in the root of the repository. A sample **hosts.ini** file:

```
[ENTERPRISE:children]
CAMPUS
DATA-CENTER
WAN
DMZ

[CAMPUS:children]
CAMPUS-CORE
CAMPUS-DISTRIBUTION
CAMPUS ACCESS

[CAMPUS-CORE]
CORE

[CAMPUS-DISTRIBUTION]
DIST01
DIST02

[CAMPUS-ACCESS:children]
CAMPUS-ACCESS-3850
CAMPUS-ACCESS-3750

[CAMPUS-ACCESS-3850]
ACCESS01
ACCESS02

[CAMPUS-ACCESS-3750]
ACCESS03

[DATA-CENTER:children]
DATA-CENTER-7K
DATA-CENTER-5K

[DATA-CENTER-7K]
DC01_7K
DC02_7K

[DATA-CENTER-5K]
DC01_5K
DC02_5K

[WAN:children]
WAN-ISR
```

WAN-ACCESS

[WAN-ISR]
WANISR01

[WAN-ACCESS]
WANACCESS01

[DMZ]
DMZ01
DMZ02

Chapter 6 Network Reconnaissance

"Okay, this is the wisdom. First, time spent on reconnaissance is never wasted. Second, almost anything can be improved with the addition of bacon."
— **Jasper Fforde, Shades of Grey**

Gathering information about network devices and logical topology are the next steps to network automation. The Ansible / Cisco **ios_facts** module is used to gather platform information while the **ios_command** module is used to run commands and gather output. These are foundational steps to build upon.

Sample Enterprise Network Topology

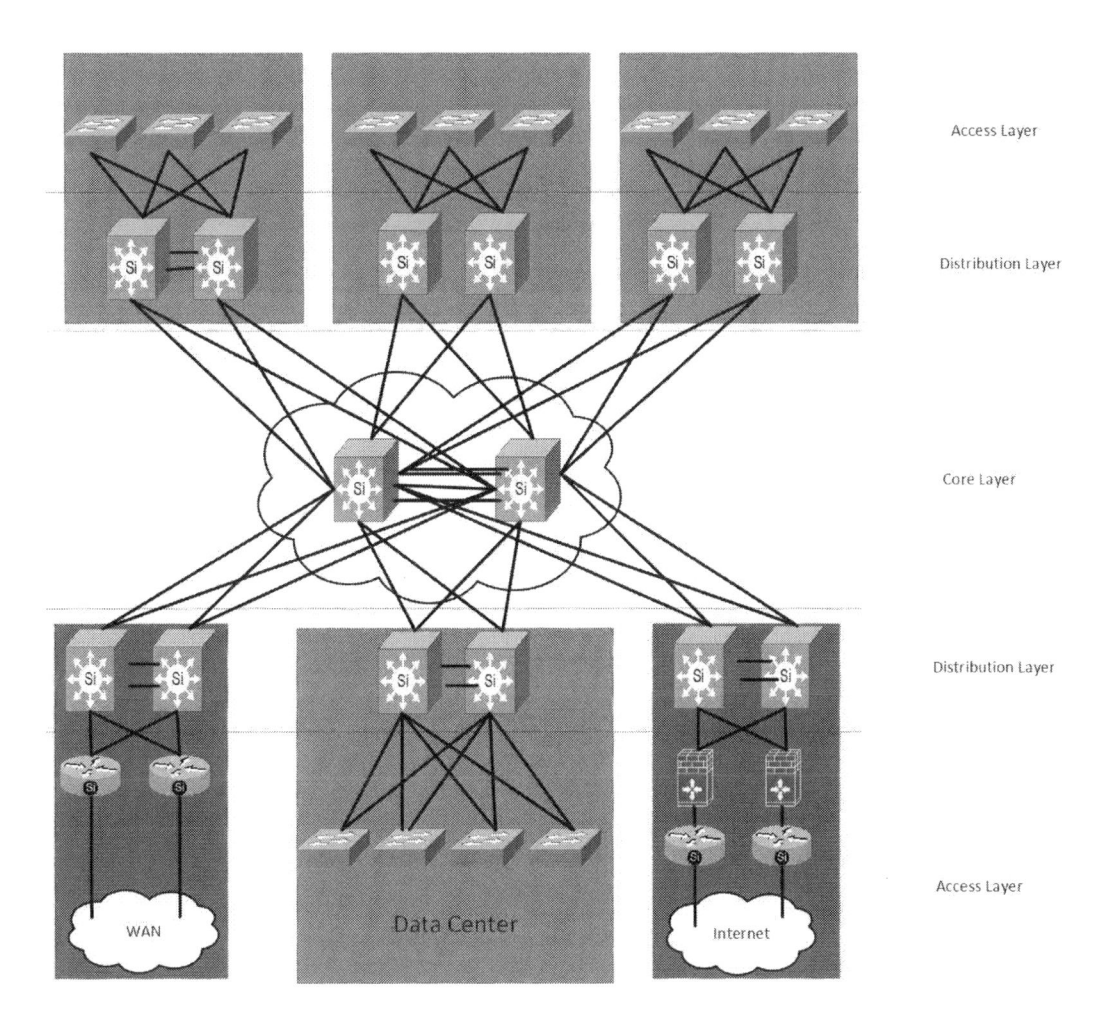

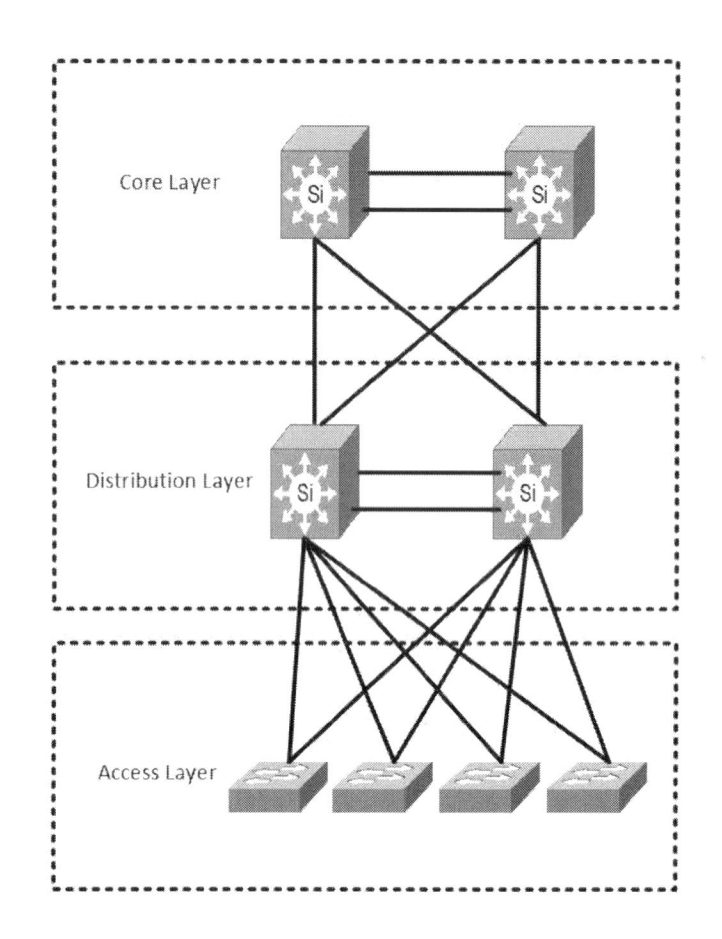

Start Gathering Information

Start automating the network!

Go to TFS.

Create a new "**Work Item**" called campus_ios_facts.

Move it to "**Active**".

Create a new branch called campus_ios_facts.

Perform a **git pull** to refresh the local repository.

Change to the **ios_facts** branch just created using **git checkout**.

* Warning *

Embedding passwords in plain text is never a good idea and is always a security concern. The following practice is not a recommended practice or best practice and there are ways, specifically **vaulting**, to protect system account passwords that provide access to the network device CLI. For the sake of educating and being able to proceed without having to fully understand and make vaulting work use this method for now. **Vaulting** also prompts for a password at run time which may interfere with full automation.

The best option is to "harden" code into a fresh repository after vaulting passwords and secrets. Migrate all folders and files, without the git history, into a fresh repository without passwords being visible. To get started either hard-code or prompt for credentials.

An alternative method is to prompt the user for credentials at run time. Hard-code the service account username and prompt for the password when the Ansible playbook is executed. This approach is secure however offers less flexibility for full automation as a password is required at run time. Ansible **vars_prompt** can be used to create interactive playbooks that prompt the user for username and password.

Be aware that as soon as Git commits the local changes the password becomes visible in the clear as part of the branch. After a pull request is merged the password becomes available in clear text as part of the master branch. **This history cannot be deleted**. It is part of the Git version control.

- Ansible vault:

  https://docs.ansible.com/ansible/2.7/user_guide/vault.html

- Using vault in playbooks:

  https://docs.ansible.com/ansible/latest/user_guide/playbooks_vault.html

- How to use vault to protect sensitive data on Ubuntu:

  https://www.digitalocean.com/community/tutorials/how-to-use-vault-to-protect-sensitive-ansible-data-on-ubuntu-16-04/

- How Ansible vault works:

  https://serversforhackers.com/c/how-ansible-vault-works/

- Ansible prompts:

  https://docs.ansible.com/ansible/latest/user_guide/playbooks_prompts.html

Navigate to **/group_vars/** and create a file called "**all.yml**" and replace the username / password with credentials that will allow Ansible to log into the devices.

```
---

ioscli:
  username: "ServiceAccount"
  password: "{{ Service Account Password}}"
  host: "{{ inventory_hostname }}"
  port: 22
```

Save, commit, annotate, and push the change to the remote branch.

Navigate to **/playbooks/campus/tactical/** and create a new file called ios_facts.yml.

Write the following Ansible playbook:

* Note *: For page space and readability the output path is simply going to be "**./results**" for all output in the examples to follow. Replace this with the longer path pointing to the "**Documentation**" folder structure created earlier. For example "**../documentation/ios/recon_playbooks/ios_facts/**".

```
---

- hosts: CAMPUS
  tasks:
    - name: IOS Facts on CAMPUS
      register: ios_facts_output
      ios_facts:
        provider: "{{ ioscli }}"
    - copy:
        content="{{ ios_facts_output | to_nice_json }}"
        dest="./results/{{ inventory_hostname }}_ios_facts_output.json"
```

First, specify the scope of the play (**hosts**) and specify two tasks. The task name is **IOS Facts on CAMPUS** (which will display during run time). Register the output to the variable named **ios_facts_output**, and the provider (**credentials**) can be found in the variable {{ **ios_cli** }}.

Copy (**copy**) the content (**content**) of the variable **ios_facts_output** and apply the filter (|) "**to_nice_json**" to the output. Send this output (**dest**) to a file called {{ **inventory_hostname** }}, a variable that will be replaced at run time with each device hostname. Finally, append and create the file with **_ios_facts_output** as a JavaScript Object Notation (JSON) file and in the JSON format.

For more information about JSON please visit:

https://www.json.org/

For more information about Ansible filters please visit:

https://docs.ansible.com/ansible/2.7/user_guide/playbooks_filters.html

Here is the playbook in action, first in a dry run in check mode:

```
[automateyournetwork@LINUX HOST]$ ansible-playbook ios_facts.yml --check
PLAY [CAMPUS] ******************************************************************

TASK [IOS Facts on CAMPUS] ****************************************************
ok: [CORE]
ok: [DIST01]
ok: [DIST02]
ok: [ACCESS01]
ok: [ACCESS02]
ok: [ACCESS03]

TASK [copy] *******************************************************************
```

```
changed: [CORE]
changed: [DIST01]
changed: [DIST02]
changed: [ACCESS01]
changed: [ACCESS02]
changed: [ACCESS03]

PLAY RECAP*********************************************************************
CORE                        : ok=2    changed=1    unreachable=0    failed=0
DIST01                      : ok=2    changed=1    unreachable=0    failed=0
DIST02                      : ok=2    changed=1    unreachable=0    failed=0
ACCESS01                    : ok=2    changed=1    unreachable=0    failed=0
ACCES302                    : ok=2    changed=1    unreachable=0    failed=0
ACCESS03                    : ok=2    changed=1    unreachable=0    failed=0
```

Review the check mode output from the playbook that executes against all hosts listed in the **[CAMPUS]** group (referencing **hosts.ini**).

The task, **[IOS Facts on CAMPUS]** is executed, serially, against the hosts. This task has run successfully (for example - **ok: [Core]**) on each host. There are no errors present in the playbook and the commands executed successfully.

Next, the task **[copy]** executes on each host creating (for example **changed: [CORE]**) new output files for each host.

The play recap shows the status of each device (**ok=2**), how many changes will be made (**changed=1**), if the device was unreachable, and how many steps, if any, failed (**failed=0**).

The text will be green for all unchanged / status of ok, change to yellow to indicate changes, and red to indicate failures or errors.

Execute the play now that it is known it will execute without errors.

```
[automateyournetwork@LINUX HOST]$ ansible-playbook ios_facts.yml

PLAY [CAMPUS]*****************************************************************

TASK [IOS Facts on CAMPUS]***************************************************
ok: [CORE]
ok: [DIST01]
ok: [DIST02]
ok: [ACCESS01]
ok: [ACCESS02]
ok: [ACCESS03]

TASK [copy]*****************************************************************
changed: [CORE]
changed: [DIST01]
changed: [DIST02]
changed: [ACCESS01]
changed: [ACCESS02]
changed: [ACCESS03]

PLAY RECAP*****************************************************************
```

```
CORE                                   : ok=2    changed=1    unreachable=0    failed=0
DIST01                                 : ok=2    changed=1    unreachable=0    failed=0
DIST02                                 : ok=2    changed=1    unreachable=0    failed=0
ACCESS01                               : ok=2    changed=1    unreachable=0    failed=0
ACCES302                               : ok=2    changed=1    unreachable=0    failed=0
ACCESS03                               : ok=2    changed=1    unreachable=0    failed=0
```

Since executing the play, it is expected that output files, per-device, using **ios_facts** and in the JSON format, will be created.

Using Git, push the output back into the repository.

```
git add *
```

```
git commit -a
```

Using the **VI** editor, press (**ESC**), and add a message to the commit. Use meaningful text, such as "**JSON output from ios_facts playbook**", in every commit submitted. These messages are part of the commit and will be visible, and very useful, in Git, VS Code, and TFS. Use (**:wq**) to save the comments.

```
git push
```

Authenticate against TFS and transfer the output files into the repository.

Using Microsoft TFS or VS Code editor review the output from the **ios_facts** playbook.

Here is a concatenated version of the JSON output collected:

```
{
    "ansible_facts": {
        "ansible_net_all_ipv4_addresses": [
          192.168.1.100,
        ],
        "ansible_net_all_ipv6_addresses": [],
        "ansible_net_filesystems": [
            "bootflash:"
        ],
        "ansible_net_gather_subset": [
            "hardware",
            "default",
            "interfaces"
        ],
        "ansible_net_hostname": "DIST01",
        "ansible_net_image": "bootflash:cat4500e-universalk9.SPA.03.06.06.E.152-
.E6.bin",
        "ansible_net_interfaces": {
            "FastEthernet1": {
                "bandwidth": 10000,
                "description": null,
                "duplex": null,
                "ipv4": [],
                "lineprotocol": "down ",
                "macaddress": "xxxx.xxxx.xxxx",
                "mediatype": null,
                "mtu": 1500,
```

```json
        "operstatus": "down",
        "type": "RP management port"
    },
    "Port-channel1": {
        "bandwidth": 10000000,
        "description": "Core Uplink",
        "duplex": null,
        "ipv4": [
            {
                "address": "172.20.100.2",
                "subnet": "30"
            }
        ],
        "lineprotocol": "up (connected) ",
        "macaddress": "xxxx.xxxx.xxxx",
        "mediatype": "N/A",
        "mtu": 1500,
        "operstatus": "up",
        "type": "EtherChannel"
    },
    "Port-channel1.10": {
        "bandwidth": 10000000,
        "description": "Core Uplink",
        "duplex": null,
        "ipv4": [
            {
                "address": "172.20.100.2",
                "subnet": 30
            }
        ],
        "lineprotocol": "up (connected) ",
        "macaddress": "xxxx.xxxx.xxxx",
        "mediatype": null,
        "mtu": 1500,
        "operstatus": "up",
        "type": "EtherChannel"
    },
    "Port-channel60": {
        "bandwidth": 20000000,
        "description": "VSL",
        "duplex": null,
        "ipv4": [],
        "lineprotocol": "up (connected) ",
        "macaddress": "xxxx.xxxx.xxxx",
        "mediatype": "N/A",
        "mtu": 1500,
        "operstatus": "up",
        "type": "EtherChannel"
    },
    "TenGigabitEthernet1/1/1": {
        "bandwidth": 10000000,
        "description": "Core Uplink",
        "duplex": null,
        "ipv4": [],
        "lineprotocol": "up (connected) ",
        "macaddress": "xxxx.xxxx.xxxx",
        "mediatype": "10GBase-SR",
```

```
            "mtu": 1500,
            "operstatus": "up",
            "type": "Ten Gigabit Ethernet Port"
        },
        "Vlan1301": {
            "bandwidth": 1000000,
            "description": "BLUE_OPZone",
            "duplex": null,
            "ipv4": [
                {
                    "address": "10.10.100.1",
                    "subnet": "24"
                }
            ],
            "lineprotocol": "up ",
            "macaddress": "xxxx.xxxx.xxxx",
            "mediatype": null,
            "mtu": 1500,
            "operstatus": "up",
            "type": "Ethernet SVI"
        },
        "ansible_net_model": "WS-C4500X-16",
        "ansible_net_serialnum": "XXXXXXXXXX",
        "ansible_net_version": "03.06.06.E"
    },
    "changed": false,
    "failed": false,        ]
}
```

This is just a sample of the output. Rich and human-readable, data-driven JSON files, per-device and regardless of scale, have now been added to the repository. The first playbook has captured incredibly useful, actionable, malleable, and dynamic information about facts on all devices on the campus network. The following has been captured automatically from each device with a single command:

- Device model number.
- Device serial number.
- IOS version.
- Hostname.
- All IP addresses on the device.
- All interface information for physical interfaces.
- All loopback interfaces.
- All VLAN interfaces (SVIs).
- All port-channels information.
- Physical or virtual interface speed, administrative status, mac address, IP address, MTU, and description.

Save, commit, comment, and push the change to the remote branch.

Change to the Linux installation and **git clone** the repository or **git pull** and refresh the repository in Linux. Checkout the working branch through **git checkout ios_facts**.

Change to the /**playbooks**/**campus**/**tactical**/ folder and run the following command to execute the playbook:

```
ansible-playbook ios_facts.yml
```

The playbook should execute and provide a dynamic status report showing its progress and when it is complete. The .json output files should be building dynamically as the play runs across the campus. When the file is complete be sure to check-in the output of the playbook.

```
Git add *
```

```
Git commit -a
```

Add meaningful commit message in VI editor.

Save the file and quit VI editor.

ESC

:wq

Use Git to push the commit into the remote repository.

```
Git push
```

Provide the Microsoft TFS credentials (typically the regular Active Directory password / Windows password).

Using VS Code browse to the folder with the .json files to review the output. Using TFS browse the branch and see the output in the browser.

When satisfied with the output and everything is working, submit a pull request, perform the change management process, and merge the first Ansible playbook, and output, into TFS. Move the work item to completed.

To wrap things up with the **ios_facts** module here are the unique returned values for this module:

Key	Returned	Description
ansible_net_all_ipv4_addresses list	When interfaces is configured	All IPv4 addresses configured on the device
ansible_net_all_ipv6_addresses list	When interfaces is configured	All IPv6 addresses configured on the device
ansible_net_config string	When config is configured	The current active configuration from the device
ansible_net_filesystems list	When hardware is configured	All file system names available on the device
ansible_net_gather_subset list	Always	The list of fact subsets collected from the device

ansible_net_hostname string	Always	The configured hostname of the device
ansible_net_image string	Always	The image file the device is running
ansible_net_interfaces dict	When interfaces is configured	A hash of all interfaces running on the system
ansible_net_memfree_mb int	When hardware is configured	The available free memory on the remote device in Mb
ansible_net_memtotal_mb int	When hardware is configured	The total memory on the remote device in Mb
ansible_net_model string	Always	The model name returned from the device
ansible_net_neighbors dict	When interfaces is configured	The list of LLDP neighbors from the remote device
ansible_net_serialnum string	Always	The serial number of the remote device
ansible_net_stacked_models list	When multiple devices are configured in a stack	The model names of each device in the stack
ansible_net_stacked_serialnums list	When multiple devices are configured in a stack	The serial numbers of each device in the stack
ansible_net_version string	Always	The operating system version running on the remote device

Please visit the Ansible documentation page for more details:

https://docs.ansible.com/ansible/latest/modules/ios_facts_module.html

Moving beyond simply gathering device facts we can now gather IOS command output. Continue collecting information from the network and build more network reconnaissance playbooks this time using the **ios_command** module. This module enables the execution of Cisco IOS **show** commands and it also collects the output to files, at scale, across the network.

Go to TFS.

Add a new "**Work Item**" to the board. Make it "**Active**".

Create a new branch called "**ios_command_running_config**".

Git pull / refresh the repository in VS Code or Linux.

Change / check out the new working branch.

Create a new tactical playbook for IOS with the following YAML code:

```
---

- name: IOS Save Running Configurations
  hosts: CAMPUS
  gather_facts: no
  tasks:
    - ios_command:
        provider: "{{ ioscli }}"
        commands: show run
      register: show_run_output
    - copy:
        content="{{ show_run_output }}"
        dest="./results/{{ inventory_hostname }}_running_config.txt"
```

Save the file in VS Code as "**ios_command_running_config.yml**".

Commit it to the branch with a similar comment to "**ios_command_running_config creation**".

Change to the Linux environment.

git pull

Ensure the right branch is in focus.

git checkout

Run the new play by changing to the **/playbooks/campus/recon/** folder.

ansible-playbook ios_command_running_configuration.yml

Observe the play:

```
[automateyournetworkj@LINUX HOST]$ ansible-playbook ios_running_config.yml

PLAY [IOS Save Running Configurations] *********************************************

TASK [ios_command]*****************************************************************
ok: [CORE]
ok: [DIST01]
ok: [DIST02]
ok: [ACCESS01]
ok: [ACCESS02]
ok: [ACCESS03]

TASK [copy]***********************************************************************
changed: [CORE]
changed: [DIST01]
changed: [DIST02]
changed: [ACCESS01]
```

```
changed: [ACCESS02]
changed: [ACCESS03]

PLAY RECAP*********************************************************************************
CORE                         : ok=2     changed=1    unreachable=0    failed=0
DIST01                       : ok=2     changed=1    unreachable=0    failed=0
DIST02                       : ok=2     changed=1    unreachable=0    failed=0
ACCESS01                     : ok=2     changed=1    unreachable=0    failed=0
ACCESS02                     : ok=2     changed=1    unreachable=0    failed=0
ACCESS03                     : ok=2     changed=1    unreachable=0    failed=0
```

When the playbook has completed successfully, use Git to save, commit, comment, and push the resulting output files into the repository.

Git add *

Git commit -a

Add comments using the VI editor, press (**ESC**), type (**:wq**) to save and exit VI.

Git push

Enter TFS credentials.

Refresh the VS Code editor / **git pull** from the command palette. Or visit TFS and view the output through the TFS file explorer. There will now be a .txt file for each device containing the running-configuration of the device. A sample of the output is below:

```
{"failed": false, "changed": false, "stdout_lines": [["Building configuration...", "",
"Current configuration : 18620 bytes", "!", "! Last configuration change at 12:37:13 EDT
Thu Aug 2 2018 by automateyournetwork", "! NVRAM config last updated at 14:06:39 EDT Fri
Oct 12 2018 by automateyournetwork", "!", "version 15.2", "no service pad", "service tcp-
  keepalives-in", "service tcp-keepalives-out", "service timestamps debug datetime msec
localtime", "service timestamps log datetime msec localtime", "service password-
encryption", "service compress-config", "service counters max age 5", "!", "hostname
DIST01"
```

While having the ability to gather every device's running-configuration is incredibly powerful the default formatting of the output makes it difficult to consume. We can transform this output to the standard human-readable running-configuration using an Ansible filter.

Limit the output to the standard output lines (**stdout_line**) and change the output format to be **nice_to_yaml**. This will improve the readability of the running-configuration output.

Edit the following line in the **ios_command_running_configuration.yml**:

```
- copy:
    content="{{ show_run_output }}"
    dest="./results/{{ inventory_hostname }}_running_config.txt"
```

To modify the output format:

```
- copy:
    content="{{ show_run_output.stdout_line | nice_to_yaml }}"
```

```
      dest="./results/{{ inventory_hostname }}_running_config.txt"
```

Re-run the Ansible playbook.

```
[automateyournetworkj@LINUX HOST]$ ansible-playbook ios_running_config.yml
```

Now a human-readable version is included in output file.

```
Building configuration...
'Current configuration : 18620 bytes'
'!'
'! Last configuration change at 12:37:13 EDT Thu Aug 2 2018 by automateyournetwork'
'! NVRAM config last updated at 14:06:39 EDT Fri Oct 12 2018 by automateyournetwork'
'!'
 version 15.2
 no service pad
 service tcp-keepalives-in
 service tcp-keepalives-out
 service timestamps debug datetime msec localtime
 service timestamps log datetime msec localtime
 service password-encryption
 service compress-config
 service counters max age 5
 '!'
 hostname DIST01
```

Submit a pull request and proceed with the change management process merging into the master branch and then deleting the working branch.

Here is another **ios_command** example:

Repeat the same outlined NDLC process: add work to the board; mark it as active; create a working branch; refresh local repository / VS Code / Linux via **git pull**; change to working branch.

Create a reconnaissance playbook called **ios_command_ospfneighbors.yml**.

```
  ---

  - hosts: CAMPUS-DIST
     tasks:
       - name: run show ospf neighbors
         ios_command:
           commands: show ip ospf neighbor
           provider: "{{ ioscli }}"
         register: ospfneighbor_result
       - set_fact: ospfneighbor={{ ospfneighbor_result.stdout_lines | to_nice_yaml }}
       - name: create log file for all devices
         file: path=./results/running_config/{{ inventory_hostname }}.all.txt
state=touch
         check_mode: no
       - name: log to file for all devices
         lineinfile:
           insertafter: EOF
           path: ./results/running_config/{{ inventory_hostname }}.all.txt
```

```
        line: '{{ item }}'
      with_items:
        - "#####{{inventory_hostname}}#####"
        - "{{ ospfneighbor }}"
      check_mode: no
  - name: create log file for each device


      file: path=./results/running_config/{{ inventory_hostname }}.txt state=touch
      check_mode: no

  - name: log to file for individual device
      lineinfile:
        insertafter: EOF
        path: ./results/{{ inventory_hostname }}.txt
        line: '{{ item }}'
      with_items:
        - "#####{{inventory_hostname}}#####"
        - "{{ ospfneighbor }}"
      check_mode: no
```

Save the file in VS Code as "**ios_command_show_ospf_neighbors.yml**".

Commit it to the branch with a similar comment to "**ios_command_ospf_neighbors creation**".

Change to the Linux environment.

git pull

Change to the right working branch.

git checkout

Run the new play by changing to the **/playbooks/campus/recon/** folder.

ansible-playbook ios_command_show_ospf_neighbors.yml.

Observe the play:

```
[automateyournetwork@LINUX]$ ansible-playbook ios_command_show_ospfneighbors.yml

PLAY [CAMPUS-DIST] *************************************************************
TASK [run show ospf neighbors]*************************************************
ok: [DIST01]
ok: [DIST01]

TASK [set_fact]***************************************************************
ok: [DIST01]
ok: [DIST01]

TASK [create log file for all devices]****************************************
ok: [DIST01]
ok: [DIST01]

TASK [log to file for all devices]********************************************
```

```
ok: [DIST01] => (item=#####DIST01#####)
ok: [DIST02] => (item=####DIST02#####)

changed: [DIST01] => (item=-    - Neighbor ID    Pri   State        Dead Time
Address      Interface
    - 1.1.1.1         0    FULL/  -     00:00:38    172.20.10.1    Port-channel1
    - 1.1.1.30        0    FULL/  -     00:00:38    172.20.10.1    Port-channel1.30
    - 1.1.1.10        0    FULL/  -     00:00:35    172.20.10.1    Port-channel1.10
    - 1.1.1.20        0    FULL/  -     00:00:34    172.20.10.1    Port-channel1.20
)

changed: [DIST02] => (item=-    - Neighbor ID    Pri   State        Dead Time
Address      Interface
    - 1.1.1.1         0    FULL/  -     00:00:35    172.20.20.1    Port-channel1
    - 1.1.1.30        0    FULL/  -     00:00:35    172.20.20.1    Port-channel1.30
    - 1.1.1.20        0    FULL/  -     00:00:37    172.20.20.1    Port-channel1.20
    - 1.1.1.10        0    FULL/  -     00:00:37    172.20.20.1    Port-channel1.10

TASK [create log file for each device]************************************************
changed: [DIST01]
changed: [DIST02]

TASK [log to file for individual device]**********************************************
changed: [DIST01] => (item=#####DIST01#####)
changed: [DIST02] => (item=####DSIT02#####)
changed: [DIST01] => (item=-    - Neighbor ID    Pri   State        Dead Time
address      Interface
    - 1.1.1.1         0    FULL/  -     00:00:30    172.20.10.1    Port-channel1
    - 1.1.1.30        0    FULL/  -     00:00:37    172.20.10.1    Port-channel1.30
    - 1.1.1.10        0    FULL/  -     00:00:34    172.20.10.1    Port-channel1.10
    - 1.1.1.20        0    FULL/  -     00:00:30    172.20.10.1    Port-channel1.20
)
changed: [DIST02] => (item=-    - Neighbor ID    Pri   State        Dead Time
Address      Interface
    - 1.1.1.1         0    FULL/  -     00:00:35    172.20.20.1    Port-channel1
    - 1.1.1.30        0    FULL/  -     00:00:35    172.20.20.1    Port-channel1.30
    - 1.1.1.20        0    FULL/  -     00:00:37    172.20.20.1    Port-channel1.20
    - 1.1.1.10        0    FULL/  -     00:00:37    172.20.20.1    Port-channel1.10
)
PLAY RECAP*****************************************************************************
DIST01                : ok=6    changed=4    unreachable=0    failed=0
DIST02                : ok=6    changed=4    unreachable=0    failed=0
```

When the playbook has completed successfully, use Git to save, commit, comment, and push the resulting output files into the repository.

`Git add *`

`Git commit -a`

Add comments using the VI editor, press (**ESC**), type (**:wq**) to save and exit VI.

`Git push`

Enter TFS credentials.

Refresh the VS Code editor / **git pull** from the command palette or visit TFS and view the output through the TFS file explorer.

Submit a pull request and proceed with the change management process merging into the master branch. Delete the working branch.

Now that a few working playbooks exist that automatically gather information from the network, start growing the library of commands. Follow a simple, repeatable process to build this library from known working playbooks:

- Create a work item.
- Create a working branch.
- **git pull** the repository. Update locally.
- Change to new working branch **(git checkout)**.
- Copy the working Ansible playbook, rename and refactor playbook.
- Test the playbook in **check mode** with **verbosity (ansible-playbook –check –v)**.
- Execute the playbook **(ansible-playbook)**.
- **git push** all output artifacts into repository.
- Pull request to merge changes into master branch.
- Delete the working branch.

Take the last play as a template that can simply be updated. Clone the file and refactor the code inside the new copy.

```
- hosts:
```

Playbook scope which can be either a group or host variable:

```
  tasks:
```

List of tasks to be executed:

```
  - name:
```

Name of task. Displayed when task executes:

```
  ios_command:
```

Command provided by module:

```
  commands:
```

IOS commands to be executed:

```
  provider:
```

Credentials of device:

```
  register:
```

Create a variable:

```
- set_fact: ={{ _result.stdout_lines | to_nice_yaml }}
```

These are variables registered for later use. Set what is held in the registered variable, typically, the standard output lines (stdout_lines) in a human-readable (to_nice_yaml)(to_nice_json) format:

```
file: path=
```

The path where the file will be created at run time. Typically invoke {{ inventory_hostname }} variable to include the device hostname as part of the file name.

```
lineinfile:
line: '{{ item }}'
  with_items:
```

Method of adding lines of data to an output file one line at a time. In this case the {{ inventory_hostname }} along with the registered output {{ ospfneighbour }} are added to the file.

A full library of **ios_command_show_.yml** files can be built over time with the most commonly used commands. Here is a short list of commands that can be automated:

- **show cdp neighbors**
- **show spanning-tree**
- **show spanning-tree blockedports**
- **show ip ospf neighbors**
- **show ip route**
- **show ip route vrf**
- **show interface**
- **show interface status**
- **show version**
- **show inventory**
- **show ip interface brief**
- **show arp**
- **show mac-address table**
- **show etherchannel summary**
- **show vlan**
- **show tech**

Summary

Information gathering playbooks are simple and safe first steps towards network automation. Over time, a library of on-demand or scheduled playbooks will be be developed. These playbooks automatically generate important information about each device on the network. In addition to automating the repetitive, time consuming, and mundane task of documenting the network, the organization starts building a data warehouse of dynamically generated output files in the repository. By collecting output from the entire network on a regular basis, a historical state view in the form of the TFS repository exists. This repository shows the exact location of changes made to the network. The only limitation is creativity and how to use the wealth of information available.

In Chapter 7 the automation engine begins to make changes to the network. Having the ability to automatically gather and document information about the state of the network is a key step before making automated changes to the network. Now the organization can build playbooks that capture and document the network's state, executes the changes, and recaptures the post-change state, all automatically. Truly revolutionary!

Chapter 7 Tactical Playbooks

"Good tactics can save even the worst strategy. Bad tactics will destroy even the best strategy."
- **George S. Patton.**

Tactical changes are often one-time in nature and have a variable footprint. Sometimes there is a need to deploy a new feature that has configuration elements on every device on the network, such as a QoS policy or Netflow collection. Other changes might be limited to multiple touch points on one or two devices. Ansible playbooks are flexible enough to handle changes of any size or scope. Start accumulating various one-time playbooks that can be cloned as reusable templates of known working code. Quickly write new playbooks based on working code in the repository. A full history of the changes these playbooks make is now available in the change control history.

Moving Towards Automated Changes

The network automation engine is being given a level of authorization to change network configurations based on the playbooks being written. Be sure that collectively everyone is ready before proceeding.

Orchestration

Before starting to write any YAML think of the primary goals such as what the organization is trying to achieve with tactical playbooks. What are the requirements for the change? Which devices are impacted? Is there a specific order of operation in which to execute the commands? Is there any output that should be gathered before, during, or after the change to validate the state of the network? How can success be measured?

Ansible executes playbooks in serial fashion providing granular control and the ability to orchestrate changes across the enterprise network. Think of the steps involved in provisioning a simple VLAN on the network.

- Distribution Layer:
    - New VLAN.
    - STP root for new VLAN.
    - New SVI for VLAN.
    - Add VLAN to port-channel facing access switch.

- Access Layer:
    - New VLAN.
    - Add VLAN to port-channel facing distribution layer.
    - Configure physical interfaces as access ports on new VLAN.

Ansible translates this intent into a fully orchestrated modular playbook that can be refactored in the future for all new Access Layer VLANs.

Network Modules

Moving beyond running IOS commands through the **ios_command** module, a different Ansible module, **ios_config**, with its own unique syntax, will be introduced. The modules are similar however **ios_config** is intended to be used to configure the device with configuration, or privileged EXEC level commands, while **ios_command** is typically reserved for running **show** commands which are non-privileged.

Process

The NDLC process remains the same for making changes to the network:

- Create work items in TFS.
- Create a working branch from the master branch for every change.
- Develop and test code.
- Commit often.
- Comment code where applicable.
- Execute playbook.
- Perform pull requests to merge approved code changes into the master branch.

Now that there could potentially be an impact to the network because of changes, the incorporation of more traditional network administration personas to evaluate the required Cisco commands is needed. How and where commands should be executed and in what order as well as the impact, if any, of the change to the network needs to be assessed. Other considerations such as outage planning for impactful changes (change window, possible fail-overs, notifications to impacted users and services, change management and approvals) as well as all test plans are required. Updates to out of repository information (NMS, diagrams, legacy documentation) as well as evidence of the new automated documentation and testing that will be performed, should be included in the approval process. Some CLI validation may be required as part of an automated change.

Orchestrate the playbook to gather information about the pre-change state of the network, execute the changes, then recollect the new post-change state of the network.

Gather Information

Here, execute some of the pre-canned network reconnaissance code or craft new, playbook-specific, information gathering code that runs before changing anything. Output these files for use in validating the change or roll back if you must back out of a change.

Execute Check Mode with Verbosity

The most powerful aspect of Ansible is the ability to run playbooks in check mode. Since changes are being made to the network, which always holds a potentially negative impact, the playbook can be executed in check mode with verbosity to identify what is changing, in what order, and on what devices.

ansible-playbook network_change.yml --check –v

Execute Playbook

After performing a dry run in check mode and validating that the intent is reflected in the output, execute the playbook and automate the network changes. Remove the check mode option and re-run the playbook. Verbosity can be enabled to provide a similar view as check mode with the detailed output of each task in the playbook and how it is executed.

ansible-playbook network_change.yml -v

Regather Information

Recollect the information about the new state of the network post-change. This output can be compared to the pre-change output to validate the success of the change and the impact the change may have on routing tables or other information on the network.

Starting Small

With risk mitigation in mind, start small. Change something like an interface description or add a VLAN to a lab machine. Explore this new process for making changes by gathering evidence of its success. Lower the fear factor and raise comfort levels with a few relatively safe and small changes.

Port Description

Updating the description on an interface introduces the syntax and how to write a safe playbook that utilizes the **ios_config** module. Follow the established process of creating a branch in TFS; using **git pull** to refresh the local repository; add the playbook; commit often; and perform a pull request back into the master branch.

```
---

- hosts: DIST01
  tasks:
  - name: Configure DIST01 Port-Channel 1 Description
    ios_config:
      lines:
        -  description Core Uplink
      parents: interface Port-channel1
      provider: "{{ ioscli }}"
```

Identify what the current configuration on DIST01 port-channel1 looks like before executing the playbook:

```
DIST01# show run int po1

interface Port-channel1
ip address 172.20.10.2 255.255.255.252
```

Now execute and observe the playbook, first in **check mode** with **verbosity** as a dry run:

```
[automateyournetwork@LINUX]$ ansible-playbook portchannel_description.yml –check -v

Using /home/automateyournetwork/Lab-
Infrastructure/playbooks/campus/tactical/ansible.cfg as config file

PLAY [DIST01]********************************************************************

TASK [Configure DIST01 Port-Channel 1 Description] *****************************
changed: [DIST01] => {"banners": {}, "changed": true, "commands": ["interface Port-
channel1", "description Core Uplink"], "updates": ["interface Port-channel1",
"description Core Uplink"]}

PLAY RECAP *********************************************************************

DIST01                    : ok=1    changed=1    unreachable=0    failed=0
```

The changes will be displayed on the device, DIST01, as well as the port-channel ("**interface Port-channel1**") as well as the exact lines of configuration that will be executed ("**description Core Uplink**").

Execute the playbook without the check mode option while leaving **verbosity** set so the changes can be observed in real-time:

```
[automateyournetwork@LINUX]$ansible-playbook portchannel_description.yml -v

Using /home/automateyournetwork/Lab-
Infrastructure/playbooks/campus/tactical/ansible.cfg as config file
PLAY [DIST01]********************************************************************

TASK [Configure DIST01 Port-Channel 1 Description] *****************************

changed: [DIST01] => {"banners": {}, "changed": true, "commands": ["interface Port-
channel1", "description Core Uplink"], "updates": ["interface Port-channel1",
"description Core Uplink"]}

PLAY RECAP *********************************************************************

DIST01                    : ok=1    changed=1    unreachable=0    failed=0
```

Check the new running-configuration of port-channel 1 on DIST01:

```
DIST01# show run int po1

interface Port-channel1
description Core Uplink
ip address 172.20.10.2 255.255.255.252
```

Breaking down the YAML file first specify the scope of the play then specify the **hosts**. In this case limit to the single host DIST01. Then list the **tasks** to run against this host. The **name** of the task will be displayed at run time when this step executes. The **parent**, where the **lines** are executed, is **interface port-channel1**. If a **parent** is not specified, the **lines** are run in the global configuration of the device. Many **lines** can be executed, serially, as a list. The **provider** holds the credentials for the device.

Provision of a VLAN

Earlier in the chapter we discussed the steps required to orchestrate the provisioning of a VLAN. Here we will convert that intent and the manual steps into a fully orchestrated playbook that will provision the VLAN as a service setting up both the distribution and access side of the network. A reminder of the intent:

- Distribution layer:
    o New VLAN.
    o STP root for new VLAN.
    o New SVI for VLAN.
    o Add VLAN to port-channel facing access switch.

- Access layer:
    o New VLAN.
    o Add VLAN to port-channel facing distribution layer.
    o Configure physical interfaces as access ports on new VLAN.

```
---

- hosts: DIST01
  tasks:
  - name: Create VLAN on DIST01
    ios_config:
      lines:
        - vlan 10
        - name GREEN_VLAN_FIRST_FLOOR
        - spanning-tree vlan 10 root primary
      provider: "{{ ioscli }}"

- hosts: DIST01
  tasks:
  - name: Add VLAN to Port-Channel 2 on DIST01
    ios_config:
      lines:
        - switchport trunk allowed vlan add 10
      parents: interface Port-channel2
      provider: "{{ ioscli }}"

- hosts: DIST01
  tasks:
  - name: Copy running-config to startup-config on DIST01
    ios_command:
      lines:
        - copy run start
      provider: "{{ ioscli }}"

- hosts: ACCESS01
  tasks:
  - name: Create VLAN on ACCESS01
    ios_config:
```

```
      lines:
        - vlan 10
        - name GREEN_OPZone
      provider: "{{ ioscli }}"

- hosts: ACCESS01
  tasks:
  - name: Add VLAN to Port-channel 1
    ios_config:
      lines:
        - switchport trunk allowed vlan add 10
      parents: interface Port-channel1
      provider: "{{ ioscli }}"

- hosts: ACCESS01
  tasks:
  - name: Place Access ports on VLAN 10
    ios_config:
      lines:
        - switchport mode access
        - switchport access vlan 10
        - spanning-tree portfast
        - no shutdown
      parents: interface range GigabitEthernet1/0/2-20
      provider: "{{ ioscli }}"

- hosts: ACCESS01
  tasks:
  - name: Copy running-config to startup-config on ACCESS01
    ios_command:
      lines:
        - copy run start
      provider: "{{ ioscli }}"
```

OSPF Point-to-Point

This next example includes a change that is disruptive to the network and downtime is unavoidable. Should the operator make an error on either end or perform the change in the wrong order it could leave the network offline until somebody visits the remote device with a console cable and restores connectivity. This is avoided with automation.

The example involves interface configurations for OSPF. There are two building distribution switches connected to the core through layer 3 port-channels. Each side of the link is logically a single interface, so this should be connected as an OSPF point-to-point connection. This is not the default configuration for layer 3 port-channels and must be configured explicitly on the interface. The default is a broadcast type for OSPF. While broadcast will still work, and connectivity will be established there are some worthwhile advantages to following best practices. If running OSPF and point-to-point connections, configure the OSPF point-to-point type under those layer 3 interfaces. The OSPF hello interval as well as the dead detection interval is much higher using P2P, adjacency time is only 2 seconds (fast) versus over 40 seconds (very slow) with P2P versus broadcast. There is one less Link State Advertisement (LSA) per 30 seconds with P2P (2) versus broadcast (3) making this an extremely important setting especially as the network scales.

After building the network we discover this "bug" or "flaw" where the default was used, and the network is using OSPF type broadcast instead of type P2P on all building uplinks.

It may be quick and safe enough to perform changes manually over two sites but that is missing the point of network automation. Even with only two sites to change it still requires the manual configuration of three devices (core plus all distribution layer devices). The correct order of operation, along with the commands on the correct interfaces, must be followed during the implementation. At scale the risk is compounded per site. This change is fully documented and included in the master branch history of reference for what the state of the network was pre and post-change.

The approach is as follows:

- Capture current state:

    ```
    show ip ospf neighbors
    ```

- Change OSPF type to P2P on all links between the core and distribution layers:

    - The port-channel on the core that connects to a specific distribution switch:

        ```
        ip ospf network point-to-point
        ```

    - Port-channel 1 on the distribution switch that connects to specific port-channel on the core:

        ```
        ip ospf network point-to-point
        ```

- Capture new state:

    ```
    show ip ospf neighbors
    ```

The OSPF neighbors' playbook is already written and can be reused. This can be called as part of this playbook to gather OSPF neighbors before and after the change to compare and validate.

Follow the NDLC which by now should be second nature. Make the new working branch, **ospf_p2p**, in TFS. Refresh the local repository and change to the working branch. Update **hosts.ini** to have a new group of devices for this playbook. This group can be removed from **hosts.ini** after the play has been completed.

```
[OSPFP2P:children]
CORE
LAB-DISTRIBUTION
```

Create a new YAML file in the tactical playbook folder called **point_to_point.yml**. The playbook needs to configure port-channel 1 of the distribution switches to be OSPF type point-to-point and then the matching core port-channel interface to also be OSPF type point-to-point. The networks will take two seconds each to converge.

Write a new playbook to capture pre and post-OSPF neighbors state. This is slightly different from the existing playbook **ios_command_show_ospf_neighbors.yml** that executes the **show ip ospf neighbor** command and dumps the output to a file.

Now prompt for a file name, "PRE-CHANGE" for the output for the **show ip ospf neighbor** command. Execute the changes, and then prompt for another file name "POST-CHANGE". Recapture the **show ip ospf neighbor** command.

First create a YAML file called **ospfneighbor_prompt.yml** and add the following lines:

```
---

    - name: run show ospf neighbors
      ios_command:
        commands: show ip ospf neighbor
        provider: "{{ ioscli }}"
      register: ospfneighbor_result

    - set_fact: ospfneighbor={{ ospfneighbor_result.stdout_lines | to_nice_yaml }}

    - name: create log file for all devices
      file: path=./results/{{ output_file }}.all.txt state=touch
      check_mode: no

    - name: log to file for all devices
      lineinfile:
        insertafter: EOF
        path: ./results/{{ output_file }}.all.txt
        line: '{{ item }}'
      with_items:
        - "#####{{inventory_hostname}}#####"
        - "{{ ospfneighbor }}"
      check_mode: no

    - name: create log file for individual device
      file: path=./results/{{ output_file }}.{{inventory_hostname}}.txt state=touch
      check_mode: no

    - name: log to file for individual device
      lineinfile:
        insertafter: EOF
        path: ./results/{{ output_file }}.{{inventory_hostname}}.txt
        line: '{{ item }}'
      with_items:
        - "#####{{inventory_hostname}}#####"
        - "{{ ospfneighbor }}"
      check_mode: no
```

Next, create the executable playbook. Prompt for a file name, execute the playbook / changes, then be prompted again for another file name for the post-change output. Create a YAML file called **ospf_point_to_point.yml** and add the following lines:

```
---

- hosts: CAMPUS
  serial: 1
  vars_prompt:
    - name: output_file
```

```
    prompt: please enter output filename
    private: no
  tasks:
  - import_tasks: ospfneighbors.yml

- hosts: DIST01
  tasks:
  - name: configure DIST01
    ios_config:
      lines:
        -  ip ospf network point-to-point
      parents: interface Port-channel1
      provider: "{{ ioscli }}"

- hosts: CORE
  tasks:
  - name: configure CORE-Po1
    ios_config:
      lines:
        -  ip ospf network point-to-point
      parents: interface Port-channel1
      provider: "{{ ioscli }}"

- hosts: DIST02
  tasks:
  - name: configure DIST02
    ios_config:
      lines:
        -  ip ospf network point-to-point
      parents: interface Port-channel1
      provider: "{{ ioscli }}"

- hosts: CORE
  tasks:
  - name: configure CORE-Po2
    ios_config:
      lines:
        -  ip ospf network point-to-point
      parents: interface Port-channel2
      provider: "{{ ioscli }}"

- hosts: CAMPUS
  serial: 1

  vars_prompt:
   - name: output_file
     prompt: please enter output filename
     private: no

  tasks:
  - import_tasks: ospfneighbors.yml
```

Execute the playbook in check mode with verbosity as a dry run. Once satisfied with the results execute the change in execute mode, being aware of the outage it will cause, observing the changes.

Check the pre and post-change output files to confirm the OSPF neighbor table matches the pre-change state.

Chapter 8 Data Models and Dynamic Templates

"War is ninety percent information."
- **Napoleon Bonaparte**

In this chapter network configurations are converted and split into variables contained inside data models and dynamic templates. First group variables are created at a platform level representing standard configurations for the distribution or access layer. Unique, host-specific information will become host variables. Data models are written in the YAML format.

Jinja2 dynamic templates are introduced at this stage. These templates are used to establish the intent-based, data-driven, golden configuration that is applied to the devices. Jinaj2 files are a mix of static text, programmatic logic, and dynamic variables. These variables are called from the group and host variables in the data models. The resulting compiled output is an intent-based golden configuration.

Data Models – Group Variables

Planning data models should take some time. These models are the structures and ultimately the variables that will be called by dynamic Jinaja2 templates. The structure is important and will dictate how to use the data logically to create working Cisco configurations. Another way to think of the group and host variables is to look at them as though they are data dictionaries made up of key-pair values and lists. Templates will access the keys-pair values and iterate over lists. Remember the examples of data that should be modeled in the group variables:

- Standard NTP, IP helper addresses for DHCP, SNMP, or syslog servers.
- Access-control lists at the distribution layer.
- QoS policies either by platform, logical function, or both.
- Banners.
- AAA configurations such as RADIUS or TACACS+ servers.
- Universal secret.
- Standard interfaces.
    - o VSS configurations for core and distribution.
    - o Standardized uplinks. For example, port-channel 1 is always used as the uplink between distribution and core.
- Domain name.
- Native VLAN.
- Multicast.
- NetFlow.
- Platform type flag / identifier.
- Other features with common code across a platform.

Here are some examples of **group_vars** for the enterprise network. Remember the scope of the data model applies to all devices under the group in **hosts.ini.** For example, a data model that applies to all devices on the network:

CAMPUS.YML

```yaml
---

global_campus_defaults:
  enable_secret: $1$pdQG$0WzLBXX2$voWhxEdsiLm11

  domain: ayn.com
  snmp_communities:
    readonly:
      type: "RO 1"
    rewrite:
      type: "RW 1"

  native_vlan: "99"

  snmp_hosts:
    10.10.100.25:
      communities:
        - RO
        - RW

    10.10.100.26:
      communities:
        - RW

  logging_hosts:
    - 10.10.100.30
    - 10.10.100.31

global_campus_dhcp_servers:

  prod:
    - 10.10.100.2
    - 10.10.100.3

  dev:
    - 10.10.200.2
    - 10.10.200.3

global_campus_access_lists:
  1:
    permit:
      - 10.10.100.50
      - 10.10.100.51
    deny:
      - "any log"

  10:
    permit:
      - any
```

For templating purposes, if **global_campus_defaults.domain** is called, the value "**ayn.com**" is returned. For a dynamic template this means coverage for the domain name in all network device configurations across the campus. This becomes standardized in the builds. In this example we have **global_campus_defaults**, **global_campus_dhcp_servers**, and **global_campus_access_lists**. Since these apply to all devices in the **[CAMPUS-DISTRIBUTION]** group in **hosts.ini** these variables are processed first and, unless overridden by another variable, such as a host variable, will remain the configured value.

The next example covers the **CAMPUS-DISTRIBUTION.YML** file. This is the data model dictionary for all devices in the **[CAMPUS-DISTRIBUTION]** group in the **hosts.ini** file. Enforce the following standards to all devices that act as distribution switches on the network:

- Standard Cisco Catalyst 4500 hardware platform.
- Standard QoS model using MQC.
- Standard port-channel 1 uplink to core.
- Standard port-channel 50 and 60 for VSS.
- Standard interface for Dual Active Detection (DAD) port.
- Standard port-channel 100 for legacy, spanned, layer 2 VLANS to the core.
- Unknown port-channel numbers / access switches downstream (variable or non-standard).

```
---

platform_defaults:
  type: 4000

platform_qos:
  class_maps:
    Qos-Scavenger:
        dscp:
          - cs1

    Qos-Priority:
        dscp:
          - ef
          - cs5
          - cs4

    Qos-SECURITY+NTWK-CTRL:
        dscp:
          - cs2
          - cs3
          - cs6
          - cs7

  policy_maps:
    QoS-OUT-PO-Members:
      classes:
        Qos-Priority:
          priority: true

        Qos-SECURITY:
          bandwidth: 25

        Qos-Scavenger:
          bandwidth: 5

        class-default:
          bandwidth: 60
          dbl: true
```

```
    QoS-OUT-PO-Access-1GE:
      classes:
        Qos-Priority:
          cir: 200000000

    QoS-OUT-PO-Core:
      classes:
        Qos-Priority:
          cir: 2000000000

    QoS-OUT-PO-Access-10GE:
      classes:
        Qos-Priority:
          cir: 2000000000

    QoS-IN:
      classes:
        Qos-Priority:
          null: true

        Qos-SECURITY:
          null: true

        Qos-Scavenger:
         null: true

        class-default:
          null: true

    QoS-IN-Legacy_VLANs:
     classes:
        class-default:
          set_default: true

platform_port_channels:
  Port-channel1:
    port_channel: 1
    description: Core Uplink
    point_to_point: true
    service_policy:
      input: QoS-IN
      output: QoS-OUT-PO-Core
    vnet_list: true
    lacp_mode: "active"

    Dist01:
      ip_address: "172.20.10.2 255.255.255.252"
      members:
        TenGigabitEthernet1/1/1:
          ip_address: false
          switchport: false
          service_policy:
            output: QoS-OUT-PO-Members
        TenGigabitEthernet2/1/1:
          ip_address: false
          switchport: false
```

```yaml
        service_policy:
          output: QoS-OUT-PO-Members
 Dist02:
    ip_address: "172.20.20.2 255.255.255.252"
    members:
      TenGigabitEthernet1/1/1:
        ip_address: false
        switchport: false
        service_policy:
          output: QoS-OUT-PO-Members

      TenGigabitEthernet2/1/1:
        ip_address: false
        switchport: false
        service_policy:
          output: QoS-OUT-PO-Members

Port-channel50:
  port_channel: 50
  description: VSL
  switchport: true
  switchport_mode: trunk
  vsl: 1
  lacp_mode: "on"
  lldp_transmit: false
  lldp_receive: false

  Dist01:
    members:
      TenGigabitEthernet1/1/15:

      TenGigabitEthernet1/1/16:

  Dist02:
    members:
      TenGigabitEthernet1/1/15:

      TenGigabitEthernet1/1/16:

Port-channel60:
  port_channel: 60
  description: VSL
  switchport: true
  switchport_mode: trunk
  vsl: 2
  lacp_mode: "on"
  lldp_transmit: false
  lldp_receive: false
  Dist01:
    members:
      TenGigabitEthernet2/1/15:

      TenGigabitEthernet2/1/16:

  Dist02:
    members:
      TenGigabitEthernet2/1/15:
```

```yaml
      TenGigabitEthernet2/1/16:

  Port-channel100:
    port_channel: 100
    description: LegacyVLANs
    switchport: true
    switchport_mode: trunk
    lacp_mode: "active"

  Dist01:
    vlans: 100,200
    service_policy:
      input: QoS-IN-Legacy_VLANs
    members:
      TenGigabitEthernet1/1/13:

      TenGigabitEthernet2/1/13:

  Dist02:
    vlans: 100,200
    service_policy:
      input: QoS-IN-Legacy_VLANs
    members:
      TenGigabitEthernet1/1/13:

      TenGigabitEthernet2/1/13:

platform_interfaces:
  Dist01:
    TenGigabitEthernet1/1/14:
      type: DAD

    TenGigabitEthernet2/1/14:
      type: DAD

  Dist02:
    TenGigabitEthernet1/1/14:
      type: DAD

    TenGigabitEthernet2/1/14:
      type: DAD
```

Data Models – Host Variables

Information that is unique to a specific device should be modeled in the host variable for that device. Follow the same standards, if possible, as **group_vars** and have a **host_defaults** section along with all the other applicable data dictionaries such as **host_vrfs**, **host_vlans**, **host_interfaces**, and **host_port_channels**. Looking at the data model for one of the distribution layer switches, DIST01, a partial configuration is started for DIST01 from the coverage provided by the [**CAMPUS-DISTRIBUTION**] **group_vars** data model. Now, complete the unique configurations specific to DIST01 using **host_vars**.

The intent is to uniquely identify the device on the network, configure the following features and options according to corporate standards, and act as a functional building distribution switch in a specific location on the campus. All multicast, vrfs, vrf list, OSPF routing, VLANs, SVIs, STP root, port-channels, and the physical interfaces on the device must be coded in the data model.

```
---

host_defaults:
  hostname: DIST01
  site_id: 100
  snmp_engineid: 10001
  snmp_server_location: BUILDING100
  boot: cat4500e-universalk9.SPA.03.06.06.E.152-2.E6.bin
host_multicast:
  pim: true
  pim_dm_fallback: false
  vrfs:
    BLUE_ZONE:
      rp_address: 10.100.255.254
      multicast_routing: true

host_vrfs:
  global:
    tag: 1
    message_digest: true
    stub: true
    networks:
      "1":
        value:
        - "172.18.100.0 0.0.0.255"
        - "172.19.100.0 0.0.0.255"

  GREEN_Zone:
    tag: 10
    message_digest: true
    stub: true
    networks:
      "10":
        value:
        - "10.101.100.0 0.0.0.255"

  RED_Zone:
    tag: 20
    message_digest: true
    stub: true
    networks:
      "20":
        value:
        - "10.102.100.0 0.0.0.255"

  BLUE_Zone:
    tag: 30
    message_digest: true
    stub: true
    networks:
      "30":
```

```
          value:
          - "10.103.0.0 0.0.255.255"

     SECURITY:
       tag: 50
       message_digest: true
       stub: true
       networks:
         "50":
           value:
           - "10.200.100.0 0.0.0.255"

host_vrf_lists:
  DIST01:
    lists:
    - SECURITY
    - GREEN_Zone
    - BLUE_Zone
    - RED_Zone

host_vlans:
    2:
     name: "In-BandManagement"

    3:
     name: WirelessAccessPoints

    100:
     name: Spanned_Legacy_VLAN01

    200:
     name: Spanned_Legacy_VLAN02

    10:
     name: BLUE_Zone_First_Floor

    11:
     name: BLUE_Zone_Voice_First_Floor

    12:
     name: BLUE_Zone_Second_Floor

    13:
     name: BLUE_Zone_Video_Second_Floor

    20:
     name: RED_Zone

    30:
     name: GREEN_Zone

    50:
     name: SECURITY
```

```
host_virtual_interfaces:

  Vlan2:
    description: "In-Band Management"
    ip_address: "172.18.100.254 255.255.255.0"

  Vlan3:
    description: "Wireless Access Points"
    ip_address: "172.19.100.1 255.255.255.0"
    ip_helper_profile: prod

  Vlan10:
    description: "BLUE_Zone_First_Floor"
    vrf: BLUE_Zone
    ip_address: "10.103.1.1 255.255.255.0"
    ip_helper_profile: prod
    message_digest_key: 00271A1507542B575F78

  Vlan11:
    description: "BLUE_Zone_Voice_First_Floor"
    vrf: BLUE_Zone
    ip_address: "10.103.129.1 255.255.255.0"
    ip_helper_profile: prod

  Vlan12:
    description: "BLUE_Zone_Second_Floor"
    vrf: BLUE_Zone
    ip_address: "10.103.2.1 255.255.255.0"
    ip_helper_profile: prod
    message_digest_key: 00271A1507542B575F78

  Vlan13:
    description: "BLUE_Zone_Voice_Second_Floor"
    vrf: BLUE_Zone
    ip_address: "10.103.130.1 255.255.255.0"
    ip_helper_profile: prod

  Vlan20:
    description: "RED_Zone"
    vrf: RED_Zone
    ip_address: "10.102.100.1 255.255.255.128"
    ip_helper_profile: prod

  Vlan30:
    description: "GREEN_Zone"
    vrf: GREEN_Zone
    ip_address: "10.101.100.1 255.255.255.128"
    ip_helper_profile: prod

  Vlan50:
    description: "SECURITY"
    vrf: SECURITY
    ip_address: "10.200.100.1 255.255.255.0"
    ip_helper_profile: prod
```

```yaml
host_spanning_tree_values:
   24576:
    - 2-3,10-13,20,30,50,100,200

host_port_channels:
  Port-channel2:
    port_channel: 2
    description: "ACCESS01 Uplink"
    switchport: true
    switchport_mode: trunk
    switchport_nonegotiate: true
    vlans: 2-3,10-11,20,30,50,100,200
    guard_root: true
    service_policy:
      input: QoS-IN
      output: QoS-OUT-PO-Access-10GE
    members:
      TenGigabitEthernet1/1/2:
        lacp: active
        service_policy:
          output: QoS-OUT-PO-Members

      TenGigabitEthernet2/1/2:
        lacp: active
        service_policy:
          output: QoS-OUT-PO-Members

  Port-channel3:
    port_channel: 3
    description: "ACCESS02 Uplink"
    switchport: true
    switchport_mode: trunk
    switchport_nonegotiate: true
    vlans: 2-3,12-13,20,30,50,100,200
    guard_root: true
    service_policy:
      input: QoS-IN
      output: QoS-OUT-PO-Access-10GE
    members:

      TenGigabitEthernet1/1/3:
        lacp: active
        service_policy:
          output: QoS-OUT-PO-Members

      TenGigabitEthernet2/1/3:
        lacp: active
        service_policy:
          output: QoS-OUT-PO-Members

host_interfaces:
  TenGigabitEthernet1/1/4:
    type: unused

  TenGigabitEthernet1/1/5:
    type: unused
```

```
  TenGigabitEthernet1/1/6:
    type: unused

  TenGigabitEthernet1/1/7:
    type: unused

  TenGigabitEthernet1/1/8:
    type: unused

  TenGigabitEthernet1/1/9:
   type: unused

  TenGigabitEthernet1/1/10:
    type: unused

  TenGigabitEthernet1/1/11:
    type: unused

  TenGigabitEthernet1/1/12:
    type: unused

  TenGigabitEthernet2/1/4:
    type: unused

  TenGigabitEthernet2/1/5:
    type: unused

  TenGigabitEthernet2/1/6:
    type: unused

  TenGigabitEthernet2/1/7:
    type: unused

  TenGigabitEthernet2/1/8:
    type: unused

  TenGigabitEthernet2/1/9:
    type: unused

  TenGigabitEthernet2/1/10:
    type: unused

  TenGigabitEthernet2/1/11:
    type: unused

  TenGigabitEthernet2/1/12:
    type: unused
```

Create Templates

The next step is to build dynamic templates. Now that a data dictionary, comprised of key-pair values along with structured lists, exists, templates can be created. The Jinja2 templates substitutes portions of configuration commands with dynamic data from the dictionary for a device or group of devices.

Exact Cisco configuration commands, including syntax, nesting, and spacing, are required to develop idempotent configurations. If the spacing is off the playbook will still execute and make the changes, however during check mode or future executions of the playbook the incorrectly spaced lines of configuration will always show up as a change, even if the commands are already present on the device.

What is a Template?

Ansible uses Jinja2 templates to enable dynamic expressions and access variables in the **group_vars** and **host_vars** data dictionaries. All templates are compiled on the local Linux host at run time and then deployed to the target host. This is done to minimize the amount of information that is passed to the target device allowing only what is required to execute the playbook.

Static / Explicit Statements

With network device configurations there are a lot of static configuration commands without any real valuable information that can be abstracted into a data model. Often it is desired to explicitly execute commands and not require any dynamic data from the dictionary. Many global configurations follow this pattern. Consider the following template, the first template, **01_ios_global.j2**, which covers all devices, regardless of platform, and the global configuration commands we will explicitly run on each device:

* Important note *: All of the IP addresses, routes, and other "data" used in these examples are purely fictitious and not intended to function on a network. The format and syntax is correct however the IP address values have all been randomly picked using private IP addresses.

```
no service pad
service tcp-keepalives-in
service tcp-keepalives-out
service timestamps debug datetime msec localtime
service timestamps log datetime msec localtime
service password-encryption
service compress-config
service counters max age 5
service compress-config
no ip bootp server
diagnostic bootup level complete
errdisable recovery interval 60
aaa new-model
clock timezone est -5 0
clock summer-time EDT recurring
ip arp proxy disable
udld enable
no ip domain-lookup
vtp domain ayn
vtp mode transparent
login on-failure log
login on-success log
spanning-tree mode rapid-pvst
spanning-tree extend system-id
ip ssh version 2
no ip forward-protocol nd
no ip http server
no ip http secure-server
```

```
logging trap debugging
line con 0
 session-timeout 5
exec-timeout 20 0
 transport output none
 stopbits 1
line vty 0 4
 session-timeout 15
access-class 10 in
 exec-timeout 20 0
 privilege level 15
 transport input ssh
 transport output none
 stopbits 1
line vty 5 15
 session-timeout 15
access-class 10 in
 exec-timeout 20 0
 privilege level 15
 transport input ssh
 transport output none
 stopbits 1
```

Basic Programmatic Logic

Even a beginner can write the basic logic statements required to create dynamic templates. Having already created the data dictionary it is now a simple matter of learning and understanding the syntax required to unlock the information. The previous example, **01_ios_global.j2**, also contains some dynamic templating required to handle the various unique platform differences or to substitute dynamic information to variables. Here is the rest of the template that includes the logical statements. Note there are no spaces in the real template they have been added to help with readability:

```
hostname {{ host_defaults.hostname }}

{%  if platform_defaults.type == 6000 %}
boot system bootdisk:{{ platform_defaults.boot }}
{%  endif %}

{%  if platform_defaults.type == 4000 %}
boot system bootflash:{{ host_defaults.boot }}
{%  endif %}

{%  if host_defaults.logging_levels is defined %}
{%      for logging_level in host_defaults.logging_levels %}
{%          for logging_target in host_defaults.logging_levels[logging_level]  %}
logging {{ logging_target }} {{ logging_level }}
{%          endfor %}
{%      endfor %}
{%  endif %}

{%  if platform_defaults.type == 6000 or platform_defaults.type == 4000 %}
service compress-config
no ip bootp server
diagnostic bootup level complete
```

```
{% endif %}

{% if platform_defaults.type == 6000 or platform_defaults.type == 4000 or
platform_defaults.type == 3850 %}
redundancy mode sso
{% endif %}

enable secret 5 {{ global_campus_defaults.enable_secret }}

username admin privilege 15 secret 5 {{ global_campus_defaults.enable_secret }}

{% if platform_defaults.type == 6000 %}
platform ip cef load-sharing ip-only
platform sub-interface maximum-vlan vlan-id 2048
platform sub-interface maximum-vlan enable
platform rate-limit layer2 port-security pkt 300 burst 10
no logging event link-status boot
logging event link-status default
{% endif %}

{% if platform_defaults.type == 3750 or platform_defaults.type == 3850  %}
stack-mac persistent timer 0
{% endif %}

ip domain-name {{ global_campus_defaults.domain }}

{% if platform_defaults.type == 4000 %}
power redundancy-mode redundant
{% endif %}

{% if host_spanning_tree_values is defined %}
{%     for host_spanning_tree_value in host_spanning_tree_values %}
{%         for vlan_list in host_spanning_tree_values[host_spanning_tree_value] %}
spanning-tree vlan {{ vlan_list }} priority {{ host_spanning_tree_value }}
{%         endfor %}
{%     endfor %}
{% endif %}

{% if platform_defaults.type == 3750 %}
port-channel load-balance src-dst-ip
{% else %}

{%     if platform_defaults.type == 6000 %}
port-channel load-balance src-dst-mixed-ip-port
{%     else %}
{%         if platform_defaults.type == 4000 or platform_defaults.type == 3850 %}
port-channel load-balance src-dst-port
{%         endif %}
{%     endif %}
{% endif %}

{% for logging_host in global_campus_defaults.logging_hosts %}
logging host {{ logging_host }}
{% endfor %}
```

The template is composed of a mix of static explicit data replacement, "if" / "else" / "end if" logic, and "for" loop logic.

Every device requires a hostname. This is a good place to start looking closer at the format of the template.

```
hostname {{ host_defaults.hostname }}
```

The Cisco IOS command to configure a hostname is **hostname <desired hostname>**. This is present on every IOS device so should be set in a global or hostname template early in the configuration because it is near the top of the running-configuration. This variable is in the **host_vars** data dictionary. The dictionary is called **host_defaults** and the key-pair value is accessible as **.hostname**. A key-pair value is a set of two linked data items: a **key**, which is a unique identifier for some item of data, and the **value**, which is either the data that is identified or a pointer to the location of that data.

Here is an explicitly evaluated "if" statement:

```
{%  if platform_defaults.type == 6000 %}
boot system bootdisk:{{ platform_defaults.boot }}
{%  endif %}
```

If the value in the key-pair value **type** in the data dictionary **platform_defaults** is equal to 6000 add the following configuration line to the template. Look up the value of the **boot** key-pair value in the data dictionary **platform_defaults** and replace this variable with the information.

A more complex example:

```
{%  if platform_defaults.type == 6000 %}
port-channel load-balance src-dst-mixed-ip-port
{%  else %}
{%      if platform_defaults.type == 4000 or platform_defaults.type == 3850 %}
port-channel load-balance src-dst-port
{%      endif %}
{%  endif %}
```

First, we are evaluating the value in the key-pair value **type** in the data dictionary **platform_defaults**. If the value equals 6000 run the command **port-channel load-balance src-dst-mixed-ip-port** otherwise if the same value equals 4000 or 3850 run the command **port-channel load-balance src-dst-port**.

Here is an example of a "for" loop:

```
{%  for access_list in global_campus_access_lists %}
{%      if global_campus_access_lists[access_list].permit is defined %}
{%          for permit in global_campus_access_lists[access_list].permit %}
access-list {{ access_list }} permit {{ permit }}
{%          endfor %}
{%  endif %}
```

"For" loops can be nested:

```
{%  if host_spanning_tree_values is defined %}
{%      for host_spanning_tree_value in host_spanning_tree_values %}
{%          for vlan_list in host_spanning_tree_values[host_spanning_tree_value] %}
```

```
spanning-tree vlan {{ vlan_list }} priority {{ host_spanning_tree_value }}
{%        endfor %}
{%      endfor %}
{%  endif %}
```

This might look complicated because we have a loop nested inside another loop. Scenarios exist where it is required to nest loops. It is not that difficult if good syntax and a consistent approach is taken.

First, evaluate if a data dictionary, **host_spanning_tree_values** is defined. If so, loop through the list **host_spanning_tree_values**. Each item in the list will also be a list: **vlan_list**. Notice the syntax used in the second loop, using square brackets and the name of the list item makes it human-readable.

Ultimately it produces the line **spanning-tree vlan {{ vlan_list }} priority {{ host_spanning_tree_value }}** for each nested list item in the data dictionary. The following data model:

```
host_spanning_tree_values:
  24576:
    - 2-3,10-13,20,30,50,100,200
```

Results in the following configuration:

```
spanning-tree vlan 2-3,10-13,20,30,50,100,200 priority 24576
```

And the template allows the configuration or intent to scale as well as different priorities for different lists of VLANs.

Recommended Practices

Some general guidelines to help write templates that are human-readable and easy to change in collaboration with a full NetDevOps team:

- Use meaningful names for all files, variables, and data models.

- Differentiate between data found in **group_vars** and **host_vars** with standard prefixes on variables in data dictionaries.

- Keep templates small, modular, and focused on specific tasks, features, platforms, or technologies.

- Do not write massive one size fits all templates designed to provide full coverage of a device.

- Model data and abstract it from configurations.

- Do not nest too deep in multi-layered "for" loops or "if" statements.

- Write code in VS Code with the Jinja2 extension installed and the YAML extension installed.

- Establish best practices and share them with the team.

- After learning and developing skills, refactor code often.

- Software development is a continuous cycle of improvement.

Scope

We have created approximately 35 templates to cover all the configurations of the core, distribution, and access devices in our enterprise network. As more features arise this list is certain to grow. Pick and choose which templates apply to the network and add more, for example an EIGRP template. For more on templating please visit:

https://docs.ansible.com/ansible/2.7/user_guide/playbooks_templating.html

More Examples of Configuration Templates

Here are more examples of templates that can be refactored to fit or used directly in a network for configuration management coverage by function. The matching data model dictionaries will be posted for reference to make it easier to connect the two, however focus on the templates at this point.

VLAN

```
vlan {{ global_campus_defaults.native_vlan }}
 name NativeVLAN

{%  if host_vlans is defined %}
{%      for host_vlan in host_vlans %}
vlan {{ host_vlan }}
 name {{ host_vlans[host_vlan].name }}
{%      endfor %}
{%  endif %}
```

Data model – group_vars CAMPUS.yml

```
global_campus_defaults:
  native_vlan: 99
```

Data model – **host_vars DIST01.yml**

```
host_vlans:
   2:
    name: "In-BandManagement"

   3:
    name: WirelessAccessPoints

   100:
    name: Spanned_Legacy_VLAN01

   200:
    name: Spanned_Legacy_VLAN02

   10:
    name: BLUE_Zone_First_Floor
```

```
    11:
     name: BLUE_Zone_Voice_First_Floor

    12:
     name: BLUE_Zone_Second_Floor

    13:
     name: BLUE_Zone_Video_Second_Floor

    20:
     name: RED_Zone

    30:
     name: GREEN_Zone

    50:
     name: SECURITY
```

VRF

```
{% if platform_defaults.type == 6000 or platform_defaults.type == 4000 %}
{%    for host_vrf in host_vrfs %}
{%        if host_vrf == "global" %}
{%        else %}
vrf definition {{ host_vrf }}
{%        endif %}
{%        if host_vrf == "global" %}
{%        else %}
 vnet tag {{ host_vrfs[host_vrf].tag }}
 address-family ipv4
 exit-address-family
{%        endif %}
{%        if host_vrfs[host_vrf].multicast is defined %}
ip multicast-routing vrf {{ host_vrf }}
{%        endif %}
{%    endfor %}
{% endif %}
```

Data model – **group_vars CAMPUS-DIST.YML** and **CAMPUS-CORE.YML**

```
platform_defaults:
  type: 4000

platform_defaults:
  type: 6000
```

Data model – **host_vars DIST01.YML**

Note: Below illustrates the data holistically and abstracted from the raw configuration. Not only is the VRF modeled, the matching OSPF information is also included, as every VRF equates to a routing table. This looks at the model as a service and an intent-based view of the device.

```
 host_vrfs:
   global:
     tag: 1
```

```yaml
      message_digest: true
    stub: true
    networks:
    "1":
      value:
      - "172.18.100.0 0.0.0.255"
      - "172.19.100.0 0.0.0.255"

  GREEN_Zone:
    tag: 10
    message_digest: true
    stub: true
    networks:
      "10":
        value:
        - "10.101.100.0 0.0.0.255"

  RED_Zone:
    tag: 20
    message_digest: true
    stub: true
    networks:
      "20":
        value:
        - "10.102.100.0 0.0.0.255"

  BLUE_Zone:
    tag: 30
    message_digest: true
    stub: true
    networks:
      "30":
        value:
        - "10.103.0.0 0.0.255.255"

  SECURITY:
    tag: 50
    message_digest: true
    stub: true
    networks:
      "50":
        value:
        - "10.200.100.0 0.0.0.255"
```

OSPF

```jinja
{%  if platform_defaults.type == 6000 or platform_defaults.type == 4000 %}
{%      for host_vrf in host_vrfs %}
{%          if host_vrf == "global" %}
router ospf {{ host_vrfs[host_vrf].tag }}
{%          else %}
router ospf {{ host_vrfs[host_vrf].tag }} vrf {{ host_vrf }}
{%          endif %}
{%          if host_defaults.hostname == "CORE" %}
 router-id 1.1.1.{{ host_vrfs[host_vrf].tag }}
{%          else %}
```

```
 router-id {{ host_defaults.site_id }}.{{ host_defaults.site_id }}.{{
ost_defaults.site_id }}.{{ host_vrfs[host_vrf].tag }}
{%          endif %}
 ispf
 auto-cost reference-bandwidth 10000
 nsf ietf
{%          if host_vrfs[host_vrf].summary_addresses is defined %}
{%              for summary_address in host_vrfs[host_vrf].summary_addresses %}
 summary-address {{ summary_address }}
{%              endfor %}
{%          endif %}


{%          if platform_defaults.type == 4000 %}
{%              if host_vrfs[host_vrf].tag != 1 %}
 capability vrf-lite
{%              endif %}
{%          endif %}
{%          if host_vrfs[host_vrf].area_0 is defined %}
 area 0 authentication message-digest
{%          endif %}
{%          if host_vrfs[host_vrf].message_digest is defined %}
 area {{ host_vrfs[host_vrf].tag }} authentication message-digest
{%          endif %}
{%          if host_vrfs[host_vrf].stub is defined %}
{%              if host_defaults.hostname == "CORE" %}
 area {{ host_vrfs[host_vrf].tag }} stub {{ host_vrfs[host_vrf].stub }}
{%              else %}
 area {{ host_vrfs[host_vrf].tag }} stub
{%              endif %}
{%          endif %}
{%          if host_vrfs[host_vrf].summary is defined %}
 area {{ host_vrfs[host_vrf].tag }} range {{ host_vrfs[host_vrf].summary }} cost {{
host_vrfs[host_vrf].summary_cost }}
{%          endif %}
{%          if platform_defaults.type == 4000 %}
 passive-interface default
{%              if host_vrfs[host_vrf].tag != 1 %}
 no passive-interface Port-channel1.{{ host_vrfs[host_vrf].tag }}
{%              else %}
 no passive-interface Port-channel1
{%              endif %}
{%          endif %}
{%          if host_vrfs[host_vrf].redistribute is defined %}
 redistribute {{ host_vrfs[host_vrf].redistribute }}
{%          endif %}
{%          if host_vrfs[host_vrf].passive_interfaces is defined %}
{%              for passive_interface in host_vrfs[host_vrf].passive_interfaces %}
 passive-interface {{ passive_interface }}
{%              endfor %}
{%          endif %}
{%          if host_vrfs[host_vrf].summary_addresses is defined %}
{%              for summary_address in host_vrfs[host_vrf].summary_addresses %}
 summary-address {{ summary_address }}
{%              endfor %}
{%          endif %}
{%          if platform_defaults.type == 4000 %}
```

```
 network 172.20.{{ host_defaults.site_id }}.0 0.0.0.3 area {{ host_vrfs[host_vrf].tag
}}
{%          endif %}
{%          if host_vrfs[host_vrf].networks is defined %}
{%              for network in host_vrfs[host_vrf].networks %}
{%                  for value in host_vrfs[host_vrf].networks[network].value %}
 network {{ value }} area {{ network }}
{%                  endfor %}
{%              endfor %}
{%          endif %}
{%          if host_vrfs[host_vrf].default_originate is defined %}
 default-information originate always
{%          endif %}
{%      endfor %}
{%  endif %}
```

Static Routes

```
{%  if host_static_routes is defined %}
{%      for host_static_route in host_static_routes %}
{%          for route in host_static_routes[host_static_route].routes %}
{%              if host_static_route == "global" %}
ip route {{ route }}
{%              else %}
ip route vrf {{ host_static_route }} {{ route }}
{%              endif %}
{%          endfor %}
{%      endfor %}
{%  endif %}
```

Data model – **host_vars** file **CORE.yml**.

```
host_static_routes:
  global:
    routes:
    - "0.0.0.0 0.0.0.0 172.20.205.114 name Management_Outside_to_Firewall"
    - "192.168.100.0 255.255.192.0 172.20.200.100 name Switch_Management_Traffic"
    - "192.168.120.0 255.255.255.0 172.18.100.50 name Load_Balancer"
    - "192.168.130.0 255.255.224.0 192.168.200.132 name WAN_Management_to_Firewall"
    - "192.168.140.0 255.255.224.0 192.168.220.132 name WAN_WAPs_to_Firewall"

  GREEN_Zone:
    routes:
    - "192.168.0.0 255.252.0.0 192.168.1.100 name WAN GREEN_Zone_Transit_to_Firewall"
    - "192.168.3.0 255.255.255.0 192.168.200.100 name Voice_Transit_to_Firewall"

  WAN_Zone:
    routes:
    - "0.0.0.0 0.0.0.0 172.20.205.146 name WAN Traffic_to_AWS"
    - "10.0.0.0 255.0.0.0 172.20.205.146 name WAN Traffic to AWS"
    - "192.168.0.0 255.240.0.0 172.20.205.146 name WAN Traffic to AWS"
```

```
interface Vlan1
 no ip address
 shutdown

{%  if host_virtual_interfaces is defined %}
{%      for host_virtual_interface in host_virtual_interfaces %}
interface {{ host_virtual_interface }}
 description {{ host_virtual_interfaces[host_virtual_interface].description }}
{%          if host_virtual_interfaces[host_virtual_interface].mac_address is defined
%}
 mac-address {{ host_virtual_interfaces[host_virtual_interface].mac_address }}
{%          endif %}
{%          if host_virtual_interfaces[host_virtual_interface].vrf is defined %}
 vrf forwarding {{ host_virtual_interfaces[host_virtual_interface].vrf }}
{%          endif %}
{%          if host_virtual_interfaces[host_virtual_interface].ip_address is defined
%}
{%              if host_virtual_interfaces[host_virtual_interface].ip_address == false
%}
 no ip address
{%              else %}
 ip address {{ host_virtual_interfaces[host_virtual_interface].ip_address }}
{%              endif %}
{%          endif %}
{%          if host_virtual_interfaces[host_virtual_interface].route_map is defined %}
 ip policy route-map {{ host_virtual_interfaces[host_virtual_interface].route_map }}
{%          endif %}
{%          if host_virtual_interfaces[host_virtual_interface].ip_helper_profile is
defined %}
{%              for helper_address in
global_dhcp_servers[host_virtual_interfaces[host_virtual_interface].ip_helper_profile]
%}
 ip helper-address {{ helper_address }}
{%              endfor %}
{%          endif %}
{%          if host_virtual_interfaces[host_virtual_interface].message_digest_key is
defined %}
 ip ospf message-digest-key 1 md5 7 {{
host_virtual_interfaces[host_virtual_interface].message_digest_key }}
{%          endif %}
{%          if host_virtual_interfaces[host_virtual_interface].point_to_point is
defined %}
 ip ospf network point-to-point
{%          endif %}
{%          if host_virtual_interfaces[host_virtual_interface].pim is defined %}
 ip pim {{ host_virtual_interfaces[host_virtual_interface].pim }}
{%          endif %}
{%      endfor %}
{%  endif %}
```

Data model – **host_vars DIST01.yml** example:

```
host_virtual_interfaces:
  Vlan2:
```

```
    description: "In-Band Management"
    ip_address: "172.18.109.254 255.255.255.0"

  Vlan3:
    description: "Wireless Access Points"
    ip_address: "172.19.109.1 255.255.255.0"
    ip_helper_profile: prod


  Vlan10:
    description: "BLUE_Zone_First_Floor"
    vrf: BLUE_Zone
    ip_address: "10.109.1.1 255.255.255.0"
    ip_helper_profile: prod
    message_digest_key: 00271A1507542B575F78

  Vlan11:
    description: "BLUE_Zone_Voice_First_Floor"
    vrf: BLUE_Zone
    ip_address: "10.109.129.1 255.255.255.0"
    ip_helper_profile: prod

  Vlan12:
    description: "BLUE_Zone_Second_Floor"
    vrf: BLUE_Zone
    ip_address: "10.109.2.1 255.255.255.0"
    ip_helper_profile: prod
    message_digest_key: 00271A1507542B575F78

  Vlan13:
    description: "BLUE_Zone_Voice_Second_Floor"
    vrf: BLUE_Zone
    ip_address: "10.109.130.1 255.255.255.0"
    ip_helper_profile: prod

  Vlan20:
    description: "RED_Zone"
    vrf: RED_Zone
    ip_address: "10.103.109.1 255.255.255.128"
    ip_helper_profile: prod

  Vlan30:
    description: "GREEN_Zone"
    vrf: GREEN_Zone
    ip_address: "10.95.109.1 255.255.255.128"
    ip_helper_profile: prod

  Vlan50:
    description: "SECURITY"
    vrf: SECURITY
    ip_address: "10.200.100.1 255.255.255.0"
    ip_helper_profile: prod
```

Port-channels are treated as a service where both the port-channel and member interfaces are configured as part of the template and data model. Port-channel templates are available for both platform (**group_vars**) and host (**host_vars**) to offer maximum flexibility.

Platform

```
{%  if platform_port_channels is defined %}
{%      for platform_port_channel in platform_port_channels %}
interface {{ platform_port_channel }}
 description {{ platform_port_channels[platform_port_channel].description }}
{%          if platform_port_channels[platform_port_channel].vnet_list is defined %}
 vnet trunk list {{ inventory_hostname }}
{%          endif %}
{%          if
platform_port_channels[platform_port_channel][inventory_hostname].ip_address is
defined %}
 ip address {{
platform_port_channels[platform_port_channel][inventory_hostname].ip_address }}
{%          endif %}
{%          if
platform_port_channels[platform_port_channel][inventory_hostname].message_digest_key
is defined %}
 ip ospf message-digest-key 1 md5 7 {{
platform_port_channels[platform_port_channel][inventory_hostname].message_digest_key
}}
{%          endif %}
{%          if platform_port_channels[platform_port_channel][inventory_hostname].pim
is defined %}
 ip pim {{ platform_port_channels[platform_port_channel][inventory_hostname].pim }}
{%          endif %}
{%          if platform_port_channels[platform_port_channel].point_to_point is defined
%}
 ip ospf network point-to-point
{%          endif %}
{%          if platform_port_channels[platform_port_channel].service_policy is defined
%}
{%              if platform_port_channels[platform_port_channel].service_policy.input
is defined %}
 service-policy input {{
platform_port_channels[platform_port_channel].service_policy.input }}
{%              endif %}
{%              if platform_port_channels[platform_port_channel].service_policy.output
is defined %}
 service-policy output {{
platform_port_channels[platform_port_channel].service_policy.output }}
{%              endif %}
{%          endif %}
{%          if platform_port_channels[platform_port_channel].switchport is defined %}
{%              if platform_port_channels[platform_port_channel].switchport == true %}
 switchport
 switchport mode {{ platform_port_channels[platform_port_channel].switchport_mode }}
```

```
 switchport nonegotiate
{%               else %}
 no switchport
{%               endif %}
{%           endif %}
{%           if platform_port_channels[platform_port_channel].guard_root is defined %}
 spanning-tree guard root
{%           endif %}
{%           if platform_port_channels[platform_port_channel].ip_address is defined %}
{%               if platform_port_channels[platform_port_channel].ip_address == "false"
%}
 no ip address
{%               endif %}
{%           endif %}
{%           if platform_port_channels[platform_port_channel].vsl is defined %}
 switch virtual link {{ platform_port_channels[platform_port_channel].vsl }}
{%               if platform_defaults.type == "6000" %}
 no platform qos channel-consistency
{%           else %}
{%               endif %}
{%           endif %}
{%           for member in
platform_port_channels[platform_port_channel][inventory_hostname].members %}
interface {{ member }}
 description {{ platform_port_channels[platform_port_channel].description }}
{%           if
platform_port_channels[platform_port_channel][inventory_hostname].members[member].swit
chport is defined %}
{%               if
platform_port_channels[platform_port_channel][inventory_hostname].members[member].swit
chport == false %}
 no switchport
{%               else %}
 switchport
{%               endif %}
{%           endif %}
{%           if platform_port_channels[platform_port_channel].switchport_mode is
defined %}
 switchport mode {{ platform_port_channels[platform_port_channel].switchport_mode }}
 switchport nonegotiate
{%           endif %}
{%           if
platform_port_channels[platform_port_channel][inventory_hostname].members[member].ip_a
ddress is defined %}
{%               if
platform_port_channels[platform_port_channel][inventory_hostname].members[member].ip_a
ddress == false %}
 no ip address
{%               endif %}
{%           endif %}
{%           if platform_port_channels[platform_port_channel].cdp is defined %}
{%               if platform_port_channels[platform_port_channel].cdp == false %}
 no cdp enable
{%               endif %}
{%           endif %}
{%           if platform_port_channels[platform_port_channel].lldp_transmit is
defined %}
```

```
{%                            if platform_port_channels[platform_port_channel].lldp_transmit ==
false %}
 no lldp transmit
{%                    endif %}
{%                endif %}
{%                if platform_port_channels[platform_port_channel].lldp_receive is
defined %}
{%                            if platform_port_channels[platform_port_channel].lldp_receive ==
false %}
 no lldp receive
{%                    endif %}
{%                endif %}
 channel-group {{ platform_port_channels[platform_port_channel].port_channel }} mode
{{ platform_port_channels[platform_port_channel].lacp_mode }}
{%                if
platform_port_channels[platform_port_channel][inventory_hostname].members[member].serv
ice_policy is defined %}
{%                        if
platform_port_channels[platform_port_channel][inventory_hostname].members[member].serv
ice_policy.input is defined %}
 service-policy input {{
platform_port_channels[platform_port_channel][inventory_hostname].members[member].serv
ice_policy.input }}
{%                        endif %}
{%                        if
platform_port_channels[platform_port_channel][inventory_hostname].members[member].serv
ice_policy.output is defined %}
 service-policy output {{
platform_port_channels[platform_port_channel][inventory_hostname].members[member].serv
ice_policy.output }}
{%                        endif %}
{%                    endif %}
{%            endfor %}
{%        endfor %}
{%    endif %}
```

Data model – **group_vars CAMPUS-DIST.yml**

```
platform_port_channels:
  Port-channel1:
    port_channel: 1
    description: Core Uplink
    point_to_point: true
    service_policy:
      input: QoS-IN
      output: QoS-OUT-PO-Core
    vnet_list: true
    lacp_mode: "active"

    Dist01:
      ip_address: "172.20.10.2 255.255.255.252"
      members:
        TenGigabitEthernet1/1/1:
          ip_address: false
          switchport: false
          service_policy:
```

```
        output: QoS-OUT-PO-Members

    TenGigabitEthernet2/1/1:
      ip_address: false
      switchport: false
      service_policy:
        output: QoS-OUT-PO-Members

Dist02:
  ip_address: "172.20.20.2 255.255.255.252"
  members:
    TenGigabitEthernet1/1/1:
      ip_address: false
      switchport: false
      service_policy:
        output: QoS-OUT-PO-Members
    TenGigabitEthernet2/1/1:
      ip_address: false
      switchport: false
      service_policy:
        output: QoS-OUT-PO-Members

Port-channel50:
  port_channel: 50
  description: VSL
  switchport: true
  switchport_mode: trunk
  vsl: 1
  lacp_mode: "on"
  lldp_transmit: false
  lldp_receive: false
  Dist01:
    members:
      TenGigabitEthernet1/1/15:

      TenGigabitEthernet1/1/16:

  Dist02:
    members:
      TenGigabitEthernet1/1/15:

      TenGigabitEthernet1/1/16:

Port-channel60:
  port_channel: 60
  description: VSL
  switchport: true
  switchport_mode: trunk
  vsl: 2
  lacp_mode: "on"
  lldp_transmit: false
  lldp_receive: false
  Dist01:
    members:
      TenGigabitEthernet2/1/15:
```

```
    TenGigabitEthernet2/1/16:

  Dist02:
    members:
      TenGigabitEthernet2/1/15:

      TenGigabitEthernet2/1/16:


  Port-channel100:
    port_channel: 100
    description: LegacyVLANs
    switchport: true
    switchport_mode: trunk
    lacp_mode: "active"
    Dist01:
      vlans: 100,200
      service_policy:
        input: QoS-IN-Legacy_VLANs
      members:
        TenGigabitEthernet1/1/13:

        TenGigabitEthernet2/1/13:

    Dist02:
      vlans: 100,200
      service_policy:
        input: QoS-IN-Legacy_VLANs
      members:
        TenGigabitEthernet1/1/13:

        TenGigabitEthernet2/1/13:
```

Host

The only differences that exist between host and platform port-channels are the variable prefixes. Reuse the platform data model and refactor the variable names to reflect the host interface.

Physical Interfaces

Interfaces come in a variety of configurations and requirements. Some interfaces like dual-active detection ports are needed on VSS switches. Others are user facing ports in operational zones on the network. The following physical port types are defined for the campus network:

- Dual-active detection ports.
- Unused ports.
- Operational zone ports.
- Security ports.
- Wireless access point ports.
- Custom ports.

Operational zone ports are likely the most common port type on the campus enterprise network. These are ports where user workstations, laptops, printers, and other end user devices connect to gain access to the network. Often these ports have some basic standards applied to them to keep them as secure as possible and to offer services such as VoIP.

This sample network has several operational zone VRFs that a VLAN can be part of. Access port templates are unaware of the VRF. Only the access VLAN needs to be set on the port to put it in a zone. Therefore, only a singular template for GREEN, RED, BLUE zones is required. Apply 802.1x to the operational zone ports for security purposes.

```
{%  if host_interfaces is defined %}
{%      for host_interface in host_interfaces %}
{%          if host_interfaces[host_interface].type is defined %}
{%              if host_interfaces[host_interface].type == "OPZone" %}
interface {{ host_interface }}
 switchport mode access
 switchport nonegotiate
 switchport access vlan {{ host_interfaces[host_interface].vlan }}
{%              if host_interfaces[host_interface].voice_vlan is defined %}
 switchport voice vlan {{ host_interfaces[host_interface].voice_vlan }}
{%              if platform_defaults.type == 3750 %}
 mls qos trust device cisco-phone
 mls qos trust cos
{%              endif %}
{%              if platform_defaults.type == 3850 %}
 trust device cisco-phone
{%              endif %}
{%          endif %}
{%              if host_interfaces[host_interface].voice_vlan is defined %}
{%              else %}
 power inline never
{%              endif %}
 authentication event server dead action authorize vlan {{
host_interfaces[host_interface].vlan }}
 authentication event server dead action authorize voice
 authentication host-mode multi-domain
 authentication open
 authentication order dot1x mab
 authentication priority dot1x mab
 authentication port-control auto
 authentication periodic
 mab
 dot1x pae authenticator
 dot1x timeout quiet-period 2
 dot1x timeout tx-period 10
{%              if host_interfaces[host_interface].voice_vlan is defined or
host_interfaces[host_interface].cdp_enable is defined %}
{%              else %}
 no cdp enable
{%              endif %}
```

```
{%                        if platform_defaults.type == 3750 %}
 srr-queue bandwidth share {{ platform_qos.platform_interface_values.srr_queue_share
}}
{%                        if platform_defaults.type == 2960 %}
 srr-queue bandwidth shape {{ platform_qos.platform_interface_values.srr_queue_shape
}}
{%                        else %}
 srr-queue bandwidth shape  {{ platform_qos.platform_interface_values.srr_queue_shape
}}
{%                        endif %}
 priority-queue out
{%                        endif %}
 storm-control broadcast level 30.00
 storm-control multicast level 30.00
 no lldp transmit
 no lldp receive
 spanning-tree portfast
 spanning-tree bpduguard enable
 service-policy input PM-QoS-IN
{%                        endif %}
{%                  endif %}
{%              endfor %}
{%  endif %}
```

Security ports are different in that they use port-security and mac-sticky instead of 802.1x as they are static IP cameras that do not move.

```
{%  if host_interfaces is defined %}
{%      for host_interface in host_interfaces %}
{%          if host_interfaces[host_interface].type is defined %}
{%              if host_interfaces[host_interface].type == "SECURITY" %}
interface {{ host_interface }}
 switchport mode access
 switchport nonegotiate
 switchport access vlan {{ host_interfaces[host_interface].vlan }}
{%                if platform_defaults.type == 3750 %}
 switchport port-security violation  restrict
{%                else %}
{%                    if platform_defaults.type == 3850 %}
 switchport port-security violation restrict
{%                    endif %}
{%                endif %}
 switchport port-security mac-address sticky
 switchport port-security aging time 720
 switchport port-security aging type inactivity
 switchport port-security
{%                if host_interfaces[host_interface].port_security_maximum is
defined %}
 switchport port-security maximum {{
host_interfaces[host_interface].port_security_maximum }}
{%                endif %}
 no cdp enable
 no lldp transmit
 no lldp receive
```

```
{%                if platform_defaults.type == 3750 %}
{%                    if host_interfaces[host_interface].srr_queue_share is defined %}
 srr-queue bandwidth share {{ platform_qos.platform_interface_values.srr_queue_share
}}
{%                    if platform_defaults.type == 2960 %}
 srr-queue bandwidth shape {{ platform_qos.platform_interface_values.srr_queue_shape
}}
{%                    else %}
 srr-queue bandwidth shape  {{ platform_qos.platform_interface_values.srr_queue_shape
}}
{%                    endif %}
 priority-queue out
{%                 endif %}
{%              endif %}
 storm-control broadcast level 30.00
 storm-control multicast level 30.00
 spanning-tree portfast
 spanning-tree bpduguard enable
 service-policy input PM-QoS-IN
{%               endif %}
{%           endif %}
{%        endfor %}
{%   endif %}
```

Wireless Access Point

```
{%  if host_interfaces is defined %}
{%      for host_interface in host_interfaces %}
{%          if host_interfaces[host_interface].type is defined %}
{%              if host_interfaces[host_interface].type == "WAP" %}
interface {{ host_interface }}
 switchport mode access
 switchport nonegotiate
 switchport access vlan 3
{%              if platform_defaults.type == 3750 %}
 switchport port-security violation  restrict
{%              else %}
{%                  if platform_defaults.type == 3850 %}
 switchport port-security violation restrict
{%                  endif %}
{%              endif %}
 switchport port-security mac-address sticky
 switchport port-security aging time 720
 switchport port-security aging type inactivity
 switchport port-security
{%              if platform_defaults.type == 3750 or platform_defaults.type == 2960 %}
{%                  if host_interfaces[host_interface].srr_queue_share is defined %}
 srr-queue bandwidth share {{ platform_qos.platform_interface_values.srr_queue_share
}}
{%                  if platform_defaults.type == 2960 %}
 srr-queue bandwidth shape {{ platform_qos.platform_interface_values.srr_queue_shape
}}
{%                  else %}
 srr-queue bandwidth shape  {{ platform_qos.platform_interface_values.srr_queue_shape
}}
{%                  endif %}
```

```
 priority-queue out
{%                  endif %}
{%              endif %}
 storm-control broadcast level 30.00
 storm-control multicast level 30.00
 no lldp transmit
 no lldp receive
 spanning-tree portfast
 spanning-tree bpduguard enable
 service-policy input PM-QoS-IN
{%              endif %}
{%          endif %}
{%        endfor %}
{%  endif %}
```

Custom Interfaces

Not all interfaces will fit a predefined type or port profile since every single combination of interface sub-command does not scale. Instead, this catch-all "custom" port profile has many small "if" statements checking for flags defined under an interface in a data model. These custom cases do not define a **type** field but rather define, option-by-option, what is needed to enable and disable each field.

```
{%  if host_interfaces is defined %}
{%      for host_interface in host_interfaces %}
{%          if host_interfaces[host_interface].type is not defined %}
interface {{ host_interface }}
{%              if host_interfaces[host_interface].switchport is defined %}
{%                  if host_interfaces[host_interface].switchport == true %}
 switchport nonegotiate
{%                      if platform_defaults.type == 6000 %}
 switchport
{%                      endif %}
{%                      if host_interfaces[host_interface].switchport_mode == "access"
%}
 switchport mode access
 switchport access vlan {{ host_interfaces[host_interface].vlans }}
{%                      if platform_defaults.type == 6000 %}
 spanning-tree portfast edge
{%                      else %}
 spanning-tree portfast
{%                      endif %}
 spanning-tree bpduguard enable
{%                      else %}
 switchport mode trunk
switchport trunk native vlan {{ global_campus_defaults.native_vlan }}
 switchport trunk allowed vlan {{ host_interfaces[host_interface].vlans }}
{%                      endif %}
{%                  else %}
 no switchport
{%                  endif %}
{%              endif %}
{%              if host_defaults.poe is defined %}
{%              else %}
{%                  if power_inline is defined %}
{%                      if power_inline == false %}
```

```
 power inline never
{%                  endif %}
{%                endif %}
{%            endif %}
{%            if host_interfaces[host_interface].vrf is defined %}
 vrf forwarding {{ host_interfaces[host_interface].vrf }}
{%            endif %}
{%            if host_interfaces[host_interface].ip_address is defined %}
{%              if host_interfaces[host_interface].ip_address == false %}
 no ip address
{%              else %}
 ip address {{ host_interfaces[host_interface].ip_address }}
{%              endif %}
{%            endif %}
{%            if host_interfaces[host_interface].trust_dscp is defined %}
 mls qos trust dscp
{%            endif %}
{%            if host_interfaces[host_interface].cdp_enable is defined %}
{%              if host_interfaces[host_interface].cdp_enable == false %}
 no cdp enable
{%              endif %}
{%            endif %}
{%            if host_interfaces[host_interface].portfast_edge is defined %}
 spanning-tree portfast edge
{%            endif %}
{%            if host_interfaces[host_interface].bpdu_guard is defined %}
 spanning-tree bpduguard enable
{%            endif %}
{%            if host_interfaces[host_interface].guard_root is defined %}
 spanning-tree guard root
{%            endif %}
{%            if host_interfaces[host_interface].description is defined %}
 description {{ host_interfaces[host_interface].description }}
{%            endif %}
{%            if host_interfaces[host_interface].mac_sticky is defined %}
 switchport port-security violation  restrict
 switchport port-security mac-address sticky
 switchport port-security aging time 720
 switchport port-security aging type inactivity
 switchport port-security
{%            endif %}
{%            if platform_defaults.type == 3750 or platform_defaults.type == 2960 %}
{%              if host_interfaces[host_interface].srr_queue_share is defined %}
 srr-queue bandwidth share {{ platform_qos.platform_interface_values.srr_queue_share
}}
{%              if platform_defaults.type == 2960 %}
 srr-queue bandwidth shape {{ platform_qos.platform_interface_values.srr_queue_shape
}}
{%              else %}
 srr-queue bandwidth shape  {{ platform_qos.platform_interface_values.srr_queue_shape
}}
{%              endif %}
 priority-queue out
{%              endif %}
{%            endif %}
{%            if host_interfaces[host_interface].service_policy is defined %}
{%              if platform_defaults.type == 3850 %}
```

```
 service-policy input PM-QoS-IN
 service-policy output PM-QoS-OUT-Access
{%                  endif %}
{%                  if platform_defaults.type == 3750 %}
 service-policy input PM-QoS-IN
{%                  endif %}
{%                  if host_interfaces[host_interface].service_policy.input is defined
%}
 service-policy input {{ host_interfaces[host_interface].service_policy.input }}
{%                  endif %}
{%                  if host_interfaces[host_interface].service_policy.output is
defined %}
 service-policy output {{ host_interfaces[host_interface].service_policy.output }}
{%                  endif %}
{%              endif %}
{%              if platform_defaults.type == 3750 or platform_defaults.type == 3850 %}
{%                  if host_interfaces[host_interface].storm_control_broadcast is
defined %}
{%                      if host_interfaces[host_interface].storm_control_broadcast ==
false %}
{%                      else %}
 storm-control broadcast level 30.00
{%                      endif %}
{%                  endif %}
{%                  if host_interfaces[host_interface].storm_control_multicast is
defined %}
{%                      if host_interfaces[host_interface].storm_control_multicast ==
false %}
{%                      else %}
 storm-control multicast level 30.00
{%                      endif %}
{%                  endif %}
{%              endif %}
{%          endif %}
{%      endfor %}
{%  endif %}
```

Create Tasks

Ansible tasks include an Ansible module and reference the Jinja2 templates. These tasks are called from the Ansible playbook. A YAML task file is required for each of Jinaj2 template file. Examples of tasks:

Global Configuration

```
---

- name: Create IOS Global configuration
  ios_config:
    src: ../../templates/configurations/ios/01_ios_global.j2
    provider: "{{ ioscli }}"
  register: global_config_results
```

VRF

```
---

- name: Create IOS VRF configuration
  ios_config:
    src: ../../templates/configurations/ios/19_ios_vrfs.j2
    provider: "{{ ioscli }}"
  register: global_config_results
```

OSPF

```
---

- name: Create IOS OSPF
  ios_config:
    src: ../../templates/configurations/ios/21_ios_ospf.j2
    provider: "{{ ioscli }}"
  register: global_config_results
```

VLAN

```
---

- name: Create IOS VLAN configuration
  ios_config:
    src: ../../templates/configurations/ios/23_ios_vlan.j2
    provider: "{{ ioscli }}"
  register: global_config_results
```

Assemble Configuration Campus Task

```
---

  - name: Assembled IOS Configuration for Campus
    ios_config:
      src: '../../templates/configurations/ios_combined/assembled-config-campus.j2'
      provider: "{{ ioscli }}"
    register: global_config_results
```

ansible.cfg

Before writing playbooks, be sure to create an **ansible.cfg** file located in the same folder the Ansible playbooks reside in. Here is a sample of the **ansible.cfg** file:

```
[defaults]
host_key_checking = False
inventory=../../hosts
gathering=explicit
transport=local
```

```
retry_files_enabled = False
forks=3
filter_plugins=../../filter_plugins
```

For more information about **ansible.cfg**, and Ansible configuration in general, please visit:

https://docs.ansible.com/ansible/2.7/reference_appendices/config.html

Once this file is created it is now possible to write and execute Ansible playbooks. Three Ansible playbook examples will be demonstrated: one for automated documentation and two different versions of the same playbook (an assembled and a granular master configuration management playbook).

Task Orchestration

Following best practices on the network can lead to simplified task orchestration. Select the more optimized order of task operation and execution for playbooks and avoid wasting time running redundant or unnecessary code at various logical points in the network. If DHCP, for example, will only be hosted at the distribution layer, orchestrate the code to only run the DHCP tasks against the distribution hosts.

Chapter 9 Dynamic Intent-Based Documentation

"Incorrect documentation is often worse than no documentation."
- Bertrand Meyer

Now that the network has been converted to code the data models can be used to create dynamic, automated, documentation. All the intent-based variables in the data models can be manipulated to create documentation files for each network device on the network. An Ansible playbook is created to build automated documentation based on intent and data models: **documentation.yml**. Network documentation is automated as part of the configuration management phase. The output includes:

- Dynamically generated intent-based configuration per-device:
    - Representative of the running-configuration on the device.
    - Offline version used for comparison against online running-configuration (coverage, syntax).
    - Updated as data models or logic changes.

- Dynamically generated Markdown files:
    - Display data in a different format.
    - Automated tabular view of custom user written format that is dynamically updated.
    - .MD file format.

Markdown Format

As part of the enterprise network automation, generate dynamic documentation in Markdown format. These templates are easy to write reusing much of the template code that has already been written. These Markdown files can present full running-configurations or individual components, such as VLANs, VRFs, routes, port-channels, or physical interface configurations. These automatically generated documents scale with the network and are stored with their own history and version control in TFS.

What is Markdown Format?

Markdown is a text-to-HTML conversion tool that allows for easy to read and easy to write friendly format. Output is also very web friendly and well presented in browsers. By using much of the same logic, commands, and syntax a lot of the template code exists to create these documentation templates in Jinaj2.

For more about Markdown please visit:

https://daringfireball.net/projects/markdown/

Examples of Dynamic Documentation:

Core Documentation

```
## {{ inventory_hostname }}

**VLANs**
| VLAN   | Name     |

| -----  | ------   |

| {{ global_campus_defaults.native_vlan }} | NativeVLAN |

{% for host_vlan in host_vlans|dictsort() %}

| {{ host_vlan }} | {{ host_vlans[host_vlan].name }} |

{% endfor %}

### Running Configuration

```
{{ core_config }}

```
```

This template generates a dynamic Markdown file displaying in tabular format the variable information. In this example all VLANs followed by the full generated configuration of the device is displayed. Every variable in the data model is available to be manipulated into human-readable documentation files.

Assemble

The Ansible **assemble** module is used to combine the smaller, modular, fragmented templates and build, or assemble, them into a single Jinja2 template. The following lines indicate the source of the fragments, or Jinja2 templates, and the destination where to compile the assembled template:

```
assemble:
  src: ../../templates/configurations/ios/
  dest: '../../templates/documentation/ios/ios_combined.j2'
```

More details about the **assemble** module are available here:

https://docs.ansible.com/ansible/latest/modules/assemble_module.html

Write the following **documentation.yml** Ansible playbook to generate both the configuration file per-device as well as the Markdown documentation using the template above for the core, distribution, and access layers. Examine and breakdown the following playbook:

```
---

- hosts: CAMPUS

  tasks:
    - name: create IOS combined template
      assemble:
        src: ../../templates/configurations/ios/
```

```yaml
      dest: '../../templates/documentation/ios/ios_combined.j2'
    delegate_to: localhost
    run_once: true

  - set_fact: ios_config_file=../../configurations/ios/{{inventory_hostname}}.cfg

  - name: create running configuration per device
    template:
      src: '../../templates/documentation/ios/ios_combined.j2'
      dest: "{{ ios_config_file }}"
      trim_blocks: yes

- hosts: CAMPUS-CORE

  vars:
    c6k_config: "{{ lookup('file', ios_config_file) }}"

  tasks:

    - name: create Core documentation per device
      template:
        src: '../../templates/documentation/ios/Core_Documentation.j2'
        dest: '../../documentation/campus/{{inventory_hostname}}-intent.md'

- hosts: CAMPUS-DIST

  vars:
    c4k_config: "{{ lookup('file', ios_config_file) }}"

  tasks:

    - name: create Distribution Layer documentation per device
      template:
        src: '../../templates/documentation/ios/Distribution_Documentation.j2'
        dest: '../../documentation/campus/{{inventory_hostname}}-intent.md'

- hosts: CAMPUS-ACCESS

  vars:
    c3k_config: "{{ lookup('file', ios_config_file) }}"

  tasks:

    - name: create Access Layer documentation per device
      template:
        src: '../../templates/documentation/ios/Access_documentation.j2'
        dest: '../../documentation/campus/{{inventory_hostname}}-intent.md'
```

Here is the sample of Markdown **DIST01-intent.md** file. Remember the Jinja2 template is accessing the YAML data dictionary variables to dynamically compile this Markdown file. The documentation will automatically update any time the data model is updated:

DIST01

VLANs

VLAN	Name
99	NativeVLAN
2	In-Band Management
3	Wireless Access Points
100	Spanned_Legacy_VLAN01
200	Spanned_Legacy_VLAN02
1011	BLUE_Zone_First_Floor
1012	BLUE_Zone_Voice_First_Floor
1021	BLUE_Zone_Second_Floor
1022	BLUE_Zone_Voice_Second_Floor
2301	RED_Zone
2501	SECURITY
3301	GREEN_Zone

Running Configuration

```
 no service pad
service tcp-keepalives-in
service tcp-keepalives-out
service timestamps debug datetime msec localtime
service timestamps log datetime msec localtime
service password-encryption
service counters max age 5
```

VLANs were used as an example however it is possible to utilize the data dictionaries in the data model to manipulate the variables and template documentation files in Markdown format. A devices' VLANs, VRFs, static routes, ACLS, software version, or whatever information is present in the data dictionaries, can be templated in these dynamic documentation files.

Execute Playbook – Documentation

Now execute the playbook. The **documentation.yml** file is completely non-intrusive and non-disruptive to the network. The **ios_facts** module will gather some information from the network. Otherwise everything in the documentation playbook is building offline automated documentation based on the intent files.

Check for Idempotency

Checking for idempotency of the documentation is a quick and easy way to identify the changes being made to the data models or dynamic templates. If the output from the documentation playbook has changed and is not idempotent, it is possible to use this differential to provide change management or operations, identifying what the difference is between the documentation and the running-configuration.

ansible-playbook documentation.yml –check -v

ansible-playbook documentation.yml

Verify Output

After executing the **documentation** playbook make sure to use Git to commit all the generated output into the repository.

```
Git add *

Git commit -a

Git push
```

All the automatically, dynamically, generated documentation is now part of the repository and available to be viewed either in TFS or VS Code. Browse to the output folders holding the configuration and Markdown files, exploring and validating them for accuracy. Using these files, it is possible to confirm exactly what will be pushed to the network in advance. Use this methodology to include artifacts along with pull requests to merge changes into the master branch. These artifacts can be easily read and understood by others in the change management approval flow or used by network operations on a day-to-day basis without needing to log onto the network.

Chapter 10 Configuration Management

"The development of full artificial intelligence could spell the end of the human race....It would take off on its own, and re-design itself at an ever-increasing rate. Humans, who are limited by slow biological evolution, couldn't compete, and would be superseded."
- Stephen Hawking

Now that the intent has been documented and validated two playbooks will be created with the ambitious intent of configuring the whole enterprise campus network based on the data models and using the dynamic templates. The playbooks generate the exact same configuration however one executes all the tasks serially, offering more control and insight into the playbook while the other playbook assembles all the tasks and templates into a single change, offering more speed at execution time.

Full network configuration management builds on one-time tasks and the utilization of the **ios_command** module.

configure-campus.yml

Organized by logical task executions these tasks generate the configurations based on the compiled output of the dynamic Jinja2 templates and the group and host variable data dictionaries.

This playbook executes each task serially across each device in the campus enterprise network. Using check mode with verbosity it is possible to see what tasks are making changes on what device without executing the changes. Change validation, code troubleshooting (if a playbook fails, which task is it failing on), and documentation can all be used to understand the changes or include artifacts in approval requests to execute the playbook.

The drawback of this approach is the time the playbook takes to execute. Waiting for thirty-five tasks to run serially and individually, multiplied by the number of the devices in the campus network, might not be the most optimal way to manage network configurations. This approach is great for a deep understanding and validation of a playbook, for troubleshooting and identifying failures in playbooks, or for documenting a playbook in detail. It is not great for pushing out configurations to many devices. For that reason, use the **assemble** module.

assembled-configure-campus.yml

Using another Ansible module, **assemble**, we get the best of both worlds by having many, small modular tasks and the ability to run fast, efficient, playbooks against the network. **Assemble** does exactly that, it assembles all the files, in our case our Jinja2 templates (which is another reason we prepend our templates with a numeric order for sequence at assembly time), in a folder and creates a new, single, Jinja2 file that is the result of the assembly of all the other .j2 files.

This approach allows us to push a single, large configuration as a single task in our playbook instead of thirty-five individual tasks. It should be noted that the output and the results from either the **configure-campus.yml** or **assembled-configure-campus.yml** are the same. Having both simply provides operational flexibility.

Now that the compiled output is available to use for validation, safely move forward using the data models and dynamic templates to take full control of the network configurations. At this point they are changes that will be made in the first run of this playbook. Changes may have been performed manually to ensure parity between intent-based configurations and live running-configurations.

Either way the next playbook should be executed with caution. Use verbose check mode and limit the device scope at first to ensure there is awareness of the configuration changes the playbook will make.

First, a playbook that serially executes tasks in order device-by-device is shown. The first task is to gather facts followed by the modular configuration tasks to be performed on each device. It is important to understand these tasks run on each device in sequence as opposed to running to completion on a device, then configuring the next device. Finally, we perform a **copy running-configuration startup-configuration** command committing all changes to the device. The advantages and disadvantages to this approach are discussed after examining the playbook in action.

Campus Configuration – Serial

```
---

- hosts: CAMPUS
  tasks:
    - import_tasks: ../../tasks/configurations/ios/configure_ios_global.yml
    - import_tasks: ../../tasks/configurations/ios/configure_ios_management_source.yml
    - import_tasks: ../../tasks/configurations/ios/configure_ios_archive.yml
    - import_tasks: ../../tasks/configurations/ios/configure_ios_default_gateway.yml
    - import_tasks: ../../tasks/configurations/ios/configure_ios_snmp.yml
    - import_tasks: ../../tasks/configurations/ios/configure_ios_acls.yml
    - import_tasks: ../../tasks/configurations/ios/configure_ios_mcq_qos.yml
    - import_tasks: ../../tasks/configurations/ios/configure_ios_aaa_rsa.yml

- hosts: CAMPUS-CORE-DIST
  tasks:
    - import_tasks: ../../tasks/configurations/ios/configure_ios_vsl.yml
    - import_tasks: ../../tasks/configurations/ios/configure_ios_vrf.yml
    - import_tasks: ../../tasks/configurations/ios/configure_ios_vrf_list.yml
    - import_tasks: ../../tasks/configurations/ios/configure_ios_ospf.yml
    - import_tasks: ../../tasks/configurations/ios/configure_ios_multicast.yml
    - import_tasks:
../../tasks/configurations/ios/configure_ios_platform_interfaces_DAD.yml

- hosts: CAMPUS
  tasks:
    - import_tasks: ../../tasks/configurations/ios/configure_ios_vlan.yml
    - import_tasks: ../../tasks/configurations/ios/configure_ios_vlan_interface.yml
    - import_tasks:
../../tasks/configurations/ios/configure_ios_platform_port_channel_interface.yml
    - import_tasks:
../../tasks/configurations/ios/configure_ios_host_port_channel_interface.yml
    - import_tasks:
../../tasks/configurations/ios/configure_ios_host_interfaces_unused.yml
```

```yaml
      - import_tasks:
../../tasks/configurations/ios/configure_ios_host_interfaces_OPZone.yml
      - import_tasks:
../../tasks/configurations/ios/configure_ios_host_interfaces_SECURITY.yml
      - import_tasks:
../../tasks/configurations/ios/configure_ios_host_interfaces_WAP.yml
      - import_tasks:
../../tasks/configurations/ios/configure_ios_host_interfaces_Custom.yml

  - hosts: CAMPUS-DIST
    tasks:
      - import_tasks: ../../tasks/configurations/ios/configure_ios_dhcp.yml

  - hosts: CAMPUS-ACCESS
    tasks:
      - import_tasks: ../../tasks/configurations/ios/configure_ios_powerstack.yml
      - import_tasks: ../../tasks/configurations/ios/configure_ios_mls_qos.yml
      - import_tasks: ../../tasks/configurations/ios/configure_ios_dot1x.yml
      - import_tasks: ../../tasks/configurations/ios/configure_ios_dot1x_radius.yml

  - hosts: CAMPUS-CORE
    tasks:
      - import_tasks: ../../tasks/configurations/ios/configure_ios_6k_qos.yml
      - import_tasks: ../../tasks/configurations/ios/configure_ios_prefix_list.yml
      - import_tasks: ../../tasks/configurations/ios/configure_ios_route_maps.yml
      - import_tasks: ../../tasks/configurations/ios/configure_ios_static_routes.yml
      - import_tasks:
../../tasks/configurations/ios/configure_ios_loopback_interface.yml

  - hosts: CAMPUS
    tasks:
      - import_tasks: ../../tasks/configurations/ios/ios_copyrunstart.yml
```

Each of the tasks uses the **ios_config** module and sources one of the dynamic Jinaj2 templates. For example, here is the **configure_ios_global.yml** task:

```yaml
---

- name: Create IOS Global configuration
  ios_config:
    src: ../../templates/configurations/ios/01_ios_global.j2
    provider: "{{ ioscli }}"
    register: global_config_results
```

Make a simple change to a **host_vars** file, **DIST01.yml**, adding a VLAN just to observe the playbook's results. Assuming the playbook was fully idempotent before this change it can been seen how all future changes to the network will look.

Create a working branch, **DEMO_VLAN**, in the repository. Refresh the local repository, change to this branch, and make the following changes:

First open the **DIST01.yml** file and add a VLAN:

```
---

host_vlans:
  3999:
    name: Demo_Vlan
```

Commit this to the repository, pull the change into the Linux Ansible repository, and run the playbook in check mode with verbosity:

```
ansible-playbook configure-campus –check -v

TASK [Create IOS Global configuration] ************************************************
ok: [CORE] => {"changed": false}
ok: [DIST01] => {"changed": false}
ok: [DIST02] => {"changed": false}
ok: [ACCESS01] => {"changed": false}
ok: [ACCESS02] => {"changed": false}
ok: [ACCESS03] => {"changed": false}

TASK [Create IOS Management Source VLANs] ************************************************
ok: [CORE] => {"changed": false}
ok: [DIST01] => {"changed": false}
ok: [DIST02] => {"changed": false}
ok: [ACCESS01] => {"changed": false}
ok: [ACCESS02] => {"changed": false}
ok: [ACCESS03] => {"changed": false}

TASK [Create IOS Archives]************************************************
ok: [CORE] => {"changed": false}
ok: [DIST01] => {"changed": false}
ok: [DIST02] => {"changed": false}
ok: [ACCESS01] => {"changed": false}
ok: [ACCESS02] => {"changed": false}
ok: [ACCESS03] => {"changed": false}

TASK [Create IOS Default Gateways] ************************************************
ok: [CORE] => {"changed": false}
ok: [DIST01] => {"changed": false}
ok: [DIST02] => {"changed": false}
ok: [ACCESS01] => {"changed": false}
ok: [ACCESS02] => {"changed": false}
ok: [ACCESS03] => {"changed": false}

TASK [Create IOS SNMP]************************************************
ok: [CORE] => {"changed": false}
ok: [DIST01] => {"changed": false}
ok: [DIST02] => {"changed": false}
ok: [ACCESS01] => {"changed": false}
ok: [ACCESS02] => {"changed": false}
ok: [ACCESS03] => {"changed": false}

TASK [Create IOS ACLs]************************************************
ok: [CORE] => {"changed": false}
ok: [DIST01] => {"changed": false}
ok: [DIST02] => {"changed": false}
ok: [ACCESS01] => {"changed": false}
```

```
ok: [ACCESS02] => {"changed": false}
ok: [ACCESS03] => {"changed": false}

TASK [Create IOS MCQ QoS]*********************************************************
ok: [CORE] => {"changed": false}
ok: [DIST01] => {"changed": false}
ok: [DIST02] => {"changed": false}
ok: [ACCESS01] => {"changed": false}
ok: [ACCESS02] => {"changed": false}
ok: [ACCESS03] => {"changed": false}

TASK [Create IOS AAA RSA configuration] *****************************************
ok: [CORE] => {"changed": false}
ok: [DIST01] => {"changed": false}
ok: [DIST02] => {"changed": false}
ok: [ACCESS01] => {"changed": false}
ok: [ACCESS02] => {"changed": false}
ok: [ACCESS03] => {"changed": false}

PLAY [CAMPUS-CORE-DIST] *********************************************************

TASK [Create IOS VSL Links] ****************************************************
ok: [CORE] => {"changed": false}
ok: [DIST01] => {"changed": false}
ok: [DIST02] => {"changed": false}

TASK [Create IOS VRF configuration] ********************************************
ok: [CORE] => {"changed": false}
ok: [DIST01] => {"changed": false}
ok: [DIST02] => {"changed": false}

TASK [Create IOS VRF List configuration] **************************************
ok: [CORE] => {"changed": false}
ok: [DIST01] => {"changed": false}
ok: [DIST02] => {"changed": false}

TASK [Create IOS OSPF] *********************************************************
ok: [CORE] => {"changed": false}
ok: [DIST01] => {"changed": false}
ok: [DIST02] => {"changed": false}

TASK [Create IOS Multicast configuration] *************************************
ok: [CORE] => {"changed": false}
ok: [DIST01] => {"changed": false}
ok: [DIST02] => {"changed": false}

TASK [Create IOS Platform Interface - Dual Active Detection - configuration] *********
ok: [CORE] => {"changed": false}
ok: [DIST01] => {"changed": false}
ok: [DIST02] => {"changed": false}

PLAY [CAMPUS] *****************************************************************

TASK [Create IOS VLAN configuration] ******************************************
ok: [CORE] => {"changed": false}
```

```
changed: [DIST01] => {"banners": {}, "changed": true, "commands": ["vlan 3999", "name
Demo_vlan"], "updates": ["vlan 3999", "name Demo_vlan"]}

ok: [DIST02] => {"changed": false}
ok: [ACCESS01] => {"changed": false}
ok: [ACCESS02] => {"changed": false}
ok: [ACCESS03] => {"changed": false}

TASK [Create IOS SVI configuration] ***************************************************
ok: [CORE] => {"changed": false}
ok: [DIST01] => {"changed": false}
ok: [DIST02] => {"changed": false}
ok: [ACCESS01] => {"changed": false}
ok: [ACCESS02] => {"changed": false}
ok: [ACCESS03] => {"changed": false}

TASK [Create IOS Platform Port-Channel Interface configuration] **********************
ok: [CORE] => {"changed": false}
ok: [DIST01] => {"changed": false}
ok: [DIST02] => {"changed": false}
ok: [ACCESS01] => {"changed": false}
ok: [ACCESS02] => {"changed": false}
ok: [ACCESS03] => {"changed": false}

TASK [Create IOS Host Port-Channel Interface configuration] **************************
ok: [CORE] => {"changed": false}
ok: [DIST01] => {"changed": false}
ok: [DIST02] => {"changed": false}
ok: [ACCESS01] => {"changed": false}
ok: [ACCESS02] => {"changed": false}
ok: [ACCESS03] => {"changed": false}

TASK [Create IOS Host Interface - Unused Ports - configuration] *********************
ok: [CORE] => {"changed": false}
ok: [DIST01] => {"changed": false}
ok: [DIST02] => {"changed": false}
ok: [ACCESS01] => {"changed": false}
ok: [ACCESS02] => {"changed": false}
ok: [ACCESS03] => {"changed": false}

TASK [Create IOS Host Interface - OPZone - configuration] **************************
ok: [CORE] => {"changed": false}
ok: [DIST01] => {"changed": false}
ok: [DIST02] => {"changed": false}
ok: [ACCESS01] => {"changed": false}
ok: [ACCESS02] => {"changed": false}
ok: [ACCESS03] => {"changed": false}

TASK [Create IOS Host Interface - SECURITY - configuration] ***********************
ok: [CORE] => {"changed": false}
ok: [DIST01] => {"changed": false}
ok: [DIST02] => {"changed": false}
ok: [ACCESS01] => {"changed": false}
ok: [ACCESS02] => {"changed": false}
ok: [ACCESS03] => {"changed": false}
```

```
TASK [Create IOS Host Interface - WAP - configuration] ******************************
ok: [CORE] => {"changed": false}
ok: [DIST01] => {"changed": false}
ok: [DIST02] => {"changed": false}
ok: [ACCESS01] => {"changed": false}
ok: [ACCESS02] => {"changed": false}
ok: [ACCESS03] => {"changed": false}

TASK [Create IOS Host Interface - Custom Ports - configuration] ********************
ok: [CORE] => {"changed": false}
ok: [DIST01] => {"changed": false}
ok: [DIST02] => {"changed": false}
ok: [ACCESS01] => {"changed": false}
ok: [ACCESS02] => {"changed": false}
ok: [ACCESS03] => {"changed": false}

PLAY [CAMPUS-DIST] ****************************************************************

TASK [Create IOS DHCP Servers] **************************************************
ok: [DIST01] => {"changed": false}
ok: [DIST02] => {"changed": false}

PLAY [CAMPUS-ACCESS] **************************************************************
ok: [ACCESS01] => {"changed": false}
ok: [ACCESS02] => {"changed": false}
ok: [ACCESS03] => {"changed": false}

PLAY [CAMPUS-CORE] ****************************************************************
ok: [CORE] => {"changed": false}

PLAY [CAMPUS] *********************************************************************

TASK [Copy Run Start] ***********************************************************
ok: [CORE] => {"changed": false}
ok: [DIST01] => {"changed": false}
ok: [DIST02] => {"changed": false}
ok: [ACCESS01] => {"changed": false}
ok: [ACCESS02] => {"changed": false}
ok: [ACCESS03] => {"changed": false}

PLAY RECAP **********************************************************************
CORE              : ok=29   changed=0   unreachable=0   failed=0
DIST01            : ok=29   changed=1   unreachable=0   failed=0
DIST02            : ok=29   changed=0   unreachable=0   failed=0
ACCESS01          : ok=29   changed=0   unreachable=0   failed=0
ACCESS01          : ok=29   changed=0   unreachable=0   failed=0
ACCESS01          : ok=29   changed=0   unreachable=0   failed=0
```

The playbook is quite lengthy, verbose, and provides an opportunity to pin-point exactly which task in the playbook is being executed. It can easily be determined which task is making changes and therefore which template the configuration is being generated from. If a playbook fails it is easy to identify the faulty template or data model. The downside is obvious: each task is performed serially, and the playbook takes, relatively, a long time to execute.

One way to help limit the playbook, given only **DIST01.yml** has changes, is to use the – **limit** option on the playbook reducing the scope to just this device:

```
ansible-playbook configure-campus.yml -v -limit DIST01.yml

TASK [Create IOS Global configuration] ***********************************************
ok: [DIST01] => {"changed": false}

TASK [Create IOS Management Source VLANs] ********************************************
ok: [DIST01] => {"changed": false}

TASK [Create IOS Archives]***********************************************************
ok: [DIST01] => {"changed": false}

TASK [Create IOS Default Gateways] **************************************************
ok: [DIST01] => {"changed": false}

TASK [Create IOS SNMP]**************************************************************
ok: [DIST01] => {"changed": false}

TASK [Create IOS ACLs]*************************************************************
ok: [DIST01] => {"changed": false}

TASK [Create IOS MCQ QoS]**********************************************************
ok: [DIST01] => {"changed": false}

TASK [Create IOS AAA RSA configuration] *********************************************
ok: [DIST01] => {"changed": false}

PLAY [CAMPUS-CORE-DIST] ***********************************************************

TASK [Create IOS VSL Links] *******************************************************
ok: [DIST01] => {"changed": false}

TASK [Create IOS VRF configuration] ***********************************************
ok: [DIST01] => {"changed": false}

TASK [Create IOS VRF List configuration] ******************************************
ok: [DIST01] => {"changed": false}

TASK [Create IOS OSPF] ************************************************************
ok: [DIST01] => {"changed": false}

TASK [Create IOS Multicast configuration] *****************************************
ok: [DIST01] => {"changed": false}

TASK [Create IOS Platform Interface - Dual Active Detection - configuration] *********
ok: [DIST01] => {"changed": false}

PLAY [CAMPUS] *********************************************************************

TASK [Create IOS VLAN configuration] **********************************************

changed: [DIST01] => {"banners": {}, "changed": true, "commands": ["vlan 3999", "name
Demo_vlan"], "updates": ["vlan 3999", "name Demo_vlan"]}
```

```
TASK [Create IOS SVI configuration] **************************************************
ok: [DIST01] => {"changed": false}

TASK [Create IOS Platform Port-Channel Interface configuration] *********************
ok: [DIST01] => {"changed": false}

TASK [Create IOS Host Port-Channel Interface configuration] ************************
ok: [DIST01] => {"changed": false}

TASK [Create IOS Host Interface - Unused Ports - configuration] ********************
ok: [DIST01] => {"changed": false}

TASK [Create IOS Host Interface - OPZone - configuration] *************************
ok: [DIST01] => {"changed": false}

TASK [Create IOS Host Interface – SECURITY - configuration] ***********************
ok: [DIST01] => {"changed": false}

TASK [Create IOS Host Interface - WAP - configuration] ****************************
ok: [DIST01] => {"changed": false}

TASK [Create IOS Host Interface - Custom Ports - configuration] *******************
ok: [DIST01] => {"changed": false}

PLAY [CAMPUS-DIST] ****************************************************************

TASK [Create IOS DHCP Servers] **************************************************
ok: [DIST01] => {"changed": false}

PLAY [CAMPUS-ACCESS] **************************************************************

PLAY [CAMPUS-CORE] ****************************************************************

PLAY [CAMPUS] *********************************************************************

TASK [Copy Run Start] ***********************************************************
ok: [DIST01] => {"changed": false}

PLAY RECAP ***********************************************************************
DIST01                     : ok=29    changed=1    unreachable=0    failed=0
```

Campus Configuration – Assembled

The complete configuration management of a device, using the same templates, but utilizing a different playbook task (**assemble**) to compile a single task, can be accomplished. The advantage is that only a single configuration change is made per-device optimizing the execution time. There are a few drawbacks, primarily the loss of control over the scope of the tasks, as well as losing visibility into the playbook at execution time. First review the playbook:

```
---

- hosts: CAMPUS
  tasks:
    - name: create IOS combined template
      assemble:
```

```
        src: ../../templates/configurations/ios/
        dest: '../../templates/configurations/ios_combined/assembled-config-campus.j2'
      check_mode: no
      delegate_to: localhost
      run_once: true
  - import_tasks: ../../tasks/configurations/ios/assembled-config-campus.yml
  - import_tasks: ../../tasks/configurations/ios/ios_copyrunstart.yml
```

Observe the playbook in action:

ansible-playbook assembled-configuration-campus.yml -v -limit DIST01

```
TASK [Assembled IOS Configuration for Campus] *****************************************

changed: [DIST01] => {"banners": {}, "changed": true, "commands": ["vlan 3999", "name
Demo_vlan"], "updates": ["vlan 3999", "name Demo_vlan"]}

TASK [Copy Run Start] ****************************************************************
ok: [DIST01] => {"changed": false, "stdout": [], "stdout_lines": []}

PLAY RECAP ***************************************************************************
DIST01                   : ok=5    changed=1    unreachable=0    failed=0
```

Assembling the Ansible tasks has dramatically improved the performance and efficiency while still achieving the same goal. This **assembled-configuration-campus.yml** playbook can be scheduled for continuous deployment while the **configuration-campus.yml** playbook can be used for more granular executions. Using check mode the serially executed playbook can be used to capture the changes as part of the change request while at execution time the assembled playbook is run.

Execute Playbooks – Serial or Assembled Campus Configuration

The full network configuration management has been automated and either the **configure-campus.yml** or **assembled-configuration-campus.yml** playbook will now be able to configure every feature and setting on each device across the network. This can be a highly disruptive play so before executing it live make sure to run the playbook in check mode several times against several devices. Achieving idempotency might mean manual changes (making changes to the device to match your new intent) or at least having an understanding of all the changes the playbook will make when it runs in execute mode. The playbook will gather facts, push assembled configurations, and write the device memory to commit the change to the startup-configuration.

Moving Forward

Ideally, a fully automated, fully idempotent, network configuration management system has been achieved and has revolutionized internal processes. The organization is now following an NDLC using a centralized repository and branching strategy. All network reconnaissance, tactical changes, and network configuration management are fully automated. So, does this mean the job is done? Not quite.

What to Automate Next?

Many more components remain on the network that are still using traditional CLI or NMS methodologies. Using the same processes, technologies, and techniques, go beyond the enterprise campus network and automate the rest of the network's logical functions. Once the entire enterprise network is automated the scope can increase to include devices like load-balancers, storage arrays, Windows and Linux servers, and anything else that can be connected using SSH.

Data Center

Ansible has supported modules designed for the enterprise data center including **NXOS** modules for the Cisco Nexus platforms. Much of the code can be reused from the campus to the data center by refactoring the modules from **ios_command** and **ios_config** to **nxos_command** or **nxos_config**.

The topology in the data center may be like the campus network with a core or possibly collapsed core and distribution layer and an access layer where servers and appliances connect to the network. A whole list of new technologies and features to data models and templates become apparent. vPC, FEX, and storage protocols such as FC, FCoE, or iSCSI all need to be included in the solution.

WAN

Software-defined WAN (SD-WAN) is one of the current hot topics and trending technologies utilizing appliance NMS-based solutions. Using Ansible and the network automation framework, build your own SD-WAN migrating your WAN solution to the intent-based automated network management framework.

WANs are perfect candidates for automation as they are often cookie-cutter templates configured device-to-device with only small changes to each making it unique (hostname, management IP, etc.) on the network. There will be some unique data models and templates required for the automated WAN solution. Multiple layers to the WAN exists, including the head-end in the campus and the spokes at each office. Automated coverage can extend to each office's spokes equipment, and any switching connected behind the spokes. VPN configurations, possible encryption or IPSec configurations, routing and switching, wireless, possibly DHCP and DNS services, and other WAN specific features and technologies need to be modeled and templated.

Load-Balancers

Traditional network devices are not the only devices that can be automated. Load-balancers, particularly F5 devices running BIG-IP, have an extensive library of Ansible modules available to be leveraged. The same principals and approach can be taken with these devices to automate them as was taken with the network devices.

Once the load-balancing configurations are automated the concept of service-chaining can be introduced into the orchestration of automated playbooks. Not only can the VRF, VLAN, associated routing, port-channel, and interface configurations be automated now the organization can orchestrate the required load-balancer requirements as part of the release configuring the network holistically as a service model approach. Full integration with the organization's automated software release can be achieved ensuring the network, from Layer 1 – 4, is first deployed as part of a larger automated workflow. After the necessary network and load-balancer components have been automatically deployed, tested, and validated, the workflow can move onto the software release (setup the database, permissions, push executable package, etc.).

For more information please refer to the following links:

F5 and Ansible:

https://www.ansible.com/integrations/networks/f5/

Ansible Module Reference Guide – F5:

https://docs.ansible.com/ansible/latest/modules/list_of_network_modules.html#f5

Chapter 11 Continuous Integration / Continuous Delivery

"The question of whether a computer can think is no more interesting than the question of whether a submarine can swim."
— **Edsger W. Dijkstra**

The final phase to network automation is to continuously integrate and deliver the Ansible playbooks into the production network. CI is the software development practice adopted for network automation. CI allows for teams to collaborate on code, integrating their changes often using Git commits and pull requests, and creating automated builds whenever there are changes made to the master branch. CD expands on the CI capability and automatically releases, or pushes, the automated builds to the network on a scheduled release. This schedule could be as frequent as hourly, nightly, or weekly. The general principal of CI/CD is that developers only need to worry about making changes to the code not how to document, integrate, or release it. The CI/CD pipeline and the automation engine takes care of this for them. This often has the side-effect of removing network operations from the equation.

CI

Throughout this book it has been advocated to follow the CI software development model. CI is the practice of merging all developer working copies to a shared repository several times a day. However, at this point in the journey, a hybrid approach of automated playbooks executed by human operators has been used. The execution of the playbooks has replaced the previous steps of copy-pasting network engineer prescribed changes, by network operations staff. Now operators log into a Linux box and execute **ansible-playbook** commands to generate automated documentation and to perform network configuration management across the enterprise. The next natural step is to automate the execution of the playbooks themselves. Cron jobs or other Linux scheduling techniques can be used to automate the scheduled execution of playbooks however there is a more elegant solution and that is by integrating the playbook execution directly into the TFS CI/CD pipeline.

A great candidate for getting started with CI is the **documentation.yml** Ansible playbook. This playbook generates the configurations and documentation for the network. Automatically running the **documentation.yml** Ansible playbook every time pull requests merge changes into the master branch results in living documentation. Network changes now include all relevant and related documentation updates without operator intervention.

Microsoft Team Foundation Server

This book is not meant to provide an exhaustive training course on Microsoft TFS but rather to introduce TFS as a code repository and a CI/CD pipeline system. The more advanced and skilled staff become with TFS, the tighter the CI/CD pipeline integration becomes. Be sure to install the Ansible Microsoft Marketplace extension into TFS before continuing.

A build is software product in its final, consumable form. In traditional software this means executables or compiled code. For network automation think of a build as a point-in-time collection of all the components that make up the functional state of a network. Using TFS, first create a **New Build Definition** using the master branch as the source code for the build. Enable automated builds when changes to master branch are made and setup an Ansible extension to execute the **documentation.yml** playbook every time an automated build is triggered. Use Git to push the generated documentation into the master branch after the automated Ansible **documentation.yml** file has completed. Documentation will now accurately reflect changes made to the network. A rich version control and artifact history is available showing exactly which pull requests or commits relate to which documentation file changes.

Click the "+ **icon**" and create a new build definition.

Create new build definition

Settings

Repository source

Repository

```
◆ Lab-Infrastructure                                              ▾
```

Default branch

```
ꚜ master                                                         ▾
```

☐ Continuous integration (build whenever this branch is updated)

Default agent queue | manage queues ↗

Check the **Continuous integration** box.

Name the build **EnterpriseCampusNetwork**.

Add Tasks to the build – add an **Ansible** task.

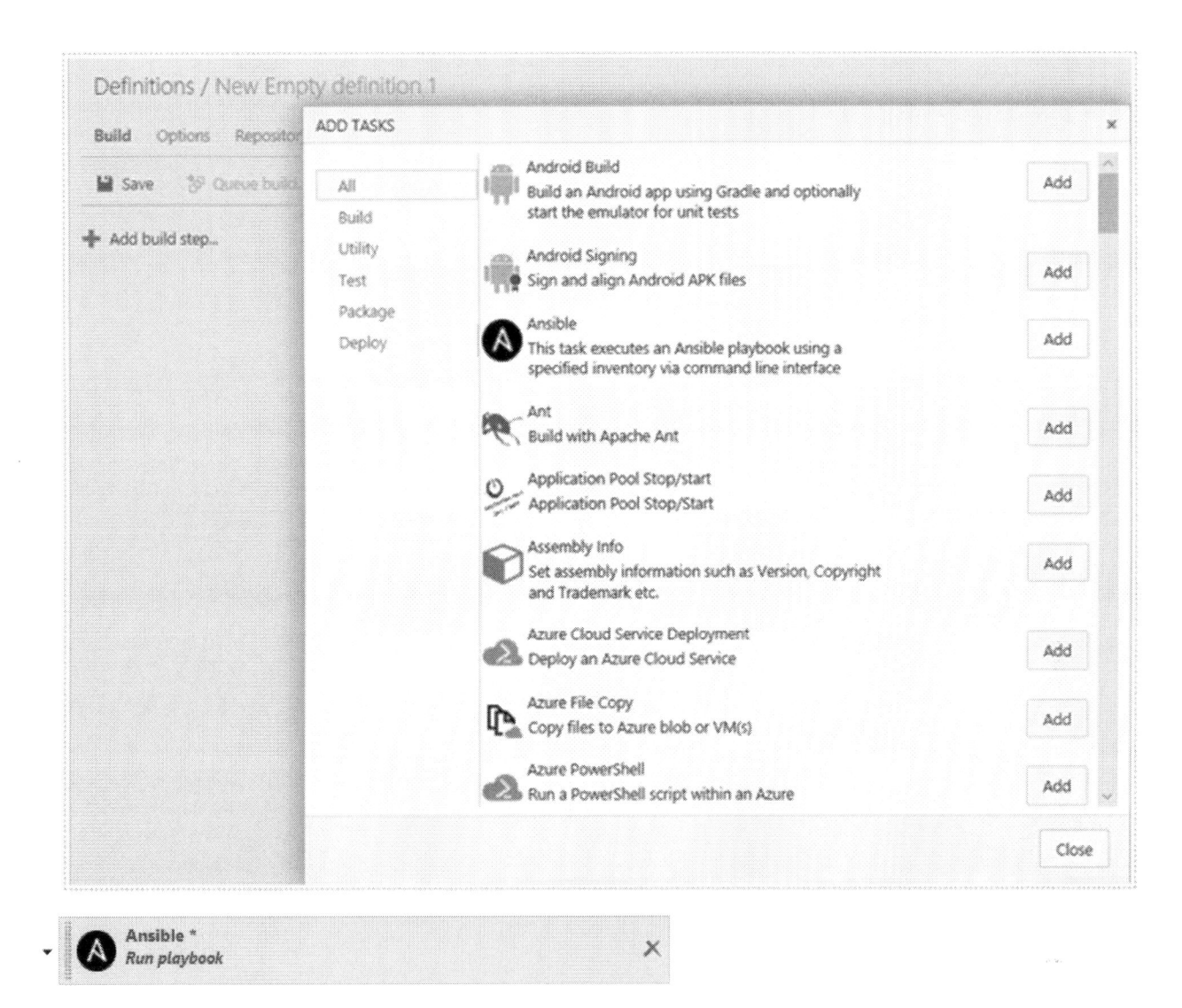

Configure the Ansible task to connect to the Linux host, specify the path of the **documentation.yml** playbook, and save the task.

Run playbook ✏

Ansible location	○ Agent machine ● Remote machine	ⓘ
Ansible SSH endpoint *	▾ ⟳ Manage ⓘ	

◢ **Playbook** *

Source	○ Agent machine ● Ansible machine	ⓘ
File path *		ⓘ

◢ **Inventory**

Inventory location	Use default inventory file ▾	ⓘ

◢ **Playbook** *

File path *	... ⓘ	

◢ **Inventory**

Inventory location	Use default inventory file ▾	ⓘ

◢ **Advanced**

Sudo	☐	ⓘ
Additional parameters		ⓘ
Fail on STDERR	☑	ⓘ

◢ **Control Options**

Enabled	☑
Continue on error	☐
Always run	☐

Now every time there is a successful pull request into the master branch, the automated documentation playbook will run and automatically refresh the documentation to reflect the changes made to the network.

Test

Automated testing of software releases, comparatively and relative to networking, can be easily integrated into the CI/CD pipeline. After the automated build and continuous integration is complete, automated testing can be triggered to release and test the software build in a test environment. This might be a development environment or pre-production environment and may involve dedicated virtual machine environments setup to receive the automated test builds. Unless a complete physical lab environment or a virtualized test environment is available, such as Jenkins or VIRL (Virtual Internet Routing Lab), automating network testing can be challenging due to the nature of networking compared to software. Software can be ported to different virtual development environments for testing while network configurations are often specific to an enterprise environment and do not easily port over to another environment. If, however, a development environment for the network exists it is possible to integrate automated testing by allowing the execution of playbooks to run against a different environment into the

NDLC. Automated testing provides another level of QA before moving to full continuous delivery of automated builds.

More information about Jenkins can be found here:

https://jenkins.io/

More information about VIRL can be found here:

http://virl.cisco.com/

CD

Continuous delivery is a software development approach where teams update software in short cycles to quickly and frequently release changes to code. Bug fixes, feature releases, and other enhancements are delivered in small modular packages more often instead of the traditional approach of accumulating changes and releasing large software packages less frequently. CD fits perfectly with network automation especially after complete network configuration management coverage and full idempotency is achieved. All future changes and all bug fixes or configuration deficiencies are added quickly and modularly, and most importantly, it is automatic as changes are merged into the master branch.

Think of the new workflow:

- Change required to the network.
- New work item created and assigned in TFS.
- New working branch created in TFS.
- Refresh local repository through **Git pull**.
- Write code in VS Code.
- Commit often.
- When ready pull request created.
- Approvals and change management.
- Pull request reviewed, approved, and merged into the master branch.
- Automated build triggered.
- All network documentation refreshed automatically to reflect change / new state.
- Automated testing occurs.
- Build passes testing.
- Automated release triggered.
- Changes delivered to production environment.
- Working branch closed.
- Analytics, change history, version control, and other metrics all available for lifecycle of change.

At no point is anyone connecting to network devices to use the CLI.

Release

Along with the enterprise software release cycle there now exists a need to establish a network release cycle. This goes beyond standard approved change windows or quarterly maintenance windows.

Determine the cadence of automated releases as well as what constitutes changes that are approved for a regular automated release cycle.

Unlike software or applications whose impact is localized to a specific application or piece of software the impact to automated network changes has a significantly larger blast radius. The closer to the network core (moving from access, and distribution, the WAN, the data center, or the DMZ) the more significant an automated change's damage can be to the network.

Some pre-approved, non-impactful, changes should be bundled into an hourly or daily release. For example:

- Changing access ports.
- Adding common features like new VLANs, port-channels, SVIs, routes, or other functions at the access and distribution layers.

Changes that impact the core or that cause a known outage or impact to the performance of the network should be scheduled as their own special release and should be released during an approved change window.

In terms of the NDLC, ideally, we want to release **assembled-configure-campus.yml** on a daily, hourly, or weekly basis. This should be triggered in TFS after the automated build, documentation, and testing, has been performed passing all quality checks built into the pipeline. The automated release is then updated to reflect the new build and is released to production on the pre-determined schedule. Putty starts to collect dust as the only reason anyone needs to connect to the CLI is to troubleshoot problems on occasion. Otherwise the enterprise network has been completely automated.

The steps to create an automated release are very similar to creating an automated deployment or automated test. Create the new release definition and add the Ansible playbook, and any other automated tasks, in sequence, then configure scheduling.

Create a **Release Definition** in TFS.

Select the **Environment**.

Add the **Ansible Tasks**.

Run playbook ✏

Ansible location	○ Agent machine ● Remote machine ⓘ
Ansible SSH endpoint *	▼ ↻ Manage ⓘ

⊿ Playbook *

Source	○ Agent machine ● Ansible machine ⓘ
File path *	ⓘ

⊿ Inventory

Inventory location	Use default inventory file ▼ ⓘ

⊿ Playbook *

File path *	⋯ ⓘ

⊿ Inventory

Inventory location	Use default inventory file ▼ ⓘ

⊿ Advanced

Sudo	☐ ⓘ
Additional parameters	ⓘ
Fail on STDERR	☑ ⓘ

⊿ Control Options

Enabled	☑
Continue on error	☐
Always run	☐

Select the **Release trigger**.

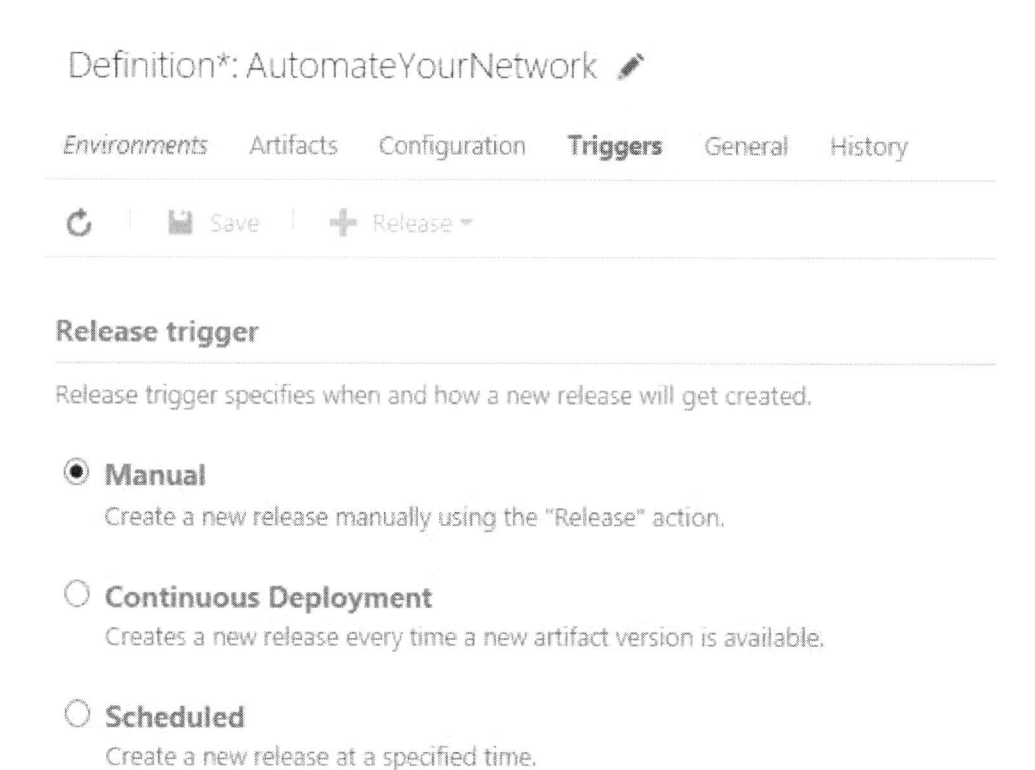

Depending on scheduled or continuously delivered releases, the configuration of the entire network has now been automated. A full release history is available within the TFS environment.

Congratulations!

Summary

"The Three Laws of Robotics:

1: A robot may not injure a human being or, through inaction, allow a human being to come to harm;
2: A robot must obey the orders given it by human beings except where such orders would conflict with the First Law;
3: A robot must protect its own existence if such protection does not conflict with the First or Second Law;
The Zeroth Law: A robot may not harm humanity, or, by inaction, allow humanity to come to harm."
— **Isaac Asimov, I, Robot**

If the "Three Laws of Robotics" as laid out by Isaac Asimov are applied, substituting humanity for the enterprise network, the basic principles and goals of automating a network becomes clear.

The robot (automation engine) may not damage the network, or, through inaction, allow the network to come to harm.

A robot must obey with the orders given it by human beings except where such orders would conflict with the first Law.

The zeroth Law: A robot may not harm the network, or, by inaction, allow the network to come to harm.

The benefits from network automation cannot, at any cost, cause network interruptions or impact to services. For the most part organizations are perfectly content running the network manually if it means stability. Should network automation impact the network negatively, especially in the early stages, those bad first impressions will be hard to recover from. Regardless of the potential time and cost savings and other benefits automation brings it absolutely cannot have the downside of causing outages or performance issues. Adopting a CI/CD NDLC, slowly progressing and evolving from network reconnaissance, to making changes to the network, to full configuration management, helps mitigate the serious risks inherent in network automation.

Development environment recap:

- Microsoft TFS:
    - Main repository.
    - Master branch.
    - Working branches.
    - Work items.
    - Pull requests.
    - Automated build.
    - Automated test.
    - Automated release.
    - CI/CD pipeline.
    - Historical view / point-in-time snapshot of network.

- Microsoft VS Code:
  - o Extensions.
  - o GUI for Git.
  - o YAML, Jinja2, Python development.

- Linux:
  - o Environment for Ansible to run.

- Git:
  - o Version control.
  - o Distributed work.
  - o Repository portability.
  - o Repository concurrency.

- Ansible:
  - o Automation framework.
  - o Playbooks.
  - o Tasks.
  - o Templates.
  - o **group_vars**.
  - o **host_vars**.

Prepare the network for connectivity requirements between VS Code, TFS, Linux, and the network devices. Service accounts should be created on the network or firewall rules added depending on the placement of the Linux and TFS hosts in relation to the network devices and VS Code clients.

The new Network Development Lifecycle (NDLC) adopted as part of a CI/CD pipeline and network automation:

- Create repository for network environment in TFS.
- Create master branch.
- Create initialization working branch.
- Clone repository to VS Code development environment.
- Clone repository to Linux Ansible environment.
- Create initial repository folder structure.
- Create **hosts.ini**.
- Commit often.
- Pull request once initial framework developed.
- Working branch per change moving forward.
- Git pull to refresh environments.
- Change into new working branch.
- Develop code.
- Git commit often.
- Pull request into master branch.
- Reviews and approvals.
- Pull request merged into the master branch.
- Automated build created.
- Automated documentation generated.
- Automated testing deployed.

- Change validated.
- Automated release scheduled.
- Branch closed.

The organization will notice an immediate impact in a variety of ways as their network administration moves towards an automated CI/CD NDLC pipeline. The agility gained in detecting or troubleshooting problems on the network, the speed and precision found in making changes or developing features and solutions and removing the network as the bottleneck in the business process, cannot be fully quantified.

While there will always be risks involved in operating a network enterprise, particularly when making changes, automating these solutions adds no more inherent risk and, in fact, it reduces or eliminates most of the manual errors involved in making changes to the network. The mix of using off the shelf, appliance or software based, NMS, and manual CLI has never done the enterprise network justice however there was, previously, no better way of doing it. The dawn of a new age in modern network administration and management has arrived in the form of network automation. Soon there will be no other way to design or operate an enterprise network. A clear competitive advantage is found in enterprises that have embraced and maximized the potential of network automation using an NDLC.

I wish you luck and success on your journey towards network automation. I hope this book provides you with the tools, methodology, and information required to get started.

- John W. Capobianco

Online Resources

GitHub

GitHub is the world's leading software development platform. GitHub brings together the world's largest community of developers to discover, share, and build better software. A GitHub repository has been setup in support of this book. Find all the playbooks, tasks, data models, and dynamic templates used in this book as well as many others in this repository.

Please visit:

https://github.com/automateyournetwork

Clone the repository locally using VS Code or the Linux host.

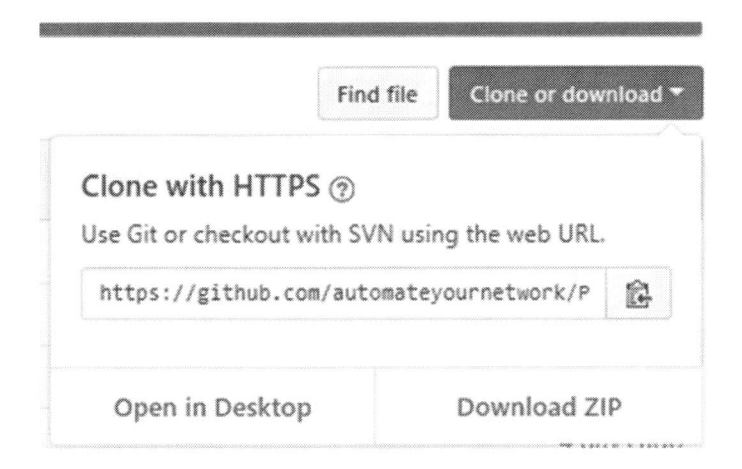

Notable GitHub Projects

Ansible:

https://github.com/ansible/ansible

Carl Buchmann – Network Engineer:

https://github.com/carlbuchmann

Jeff Geerling – Author and Software Developer:

https://github.com/geerlingguy

Trishna Guha – Senior Software Engineer, Ansible:

https://github.com/trishnaguha

Sean Cavanaugh – Builder of Networks, Ansible:

https://github.com/IPvSean

Ansible

Homepage:

https://www.ansible.com/

Documentation:

https://docs.ansible.com/

Installation:

https://docs.ansible.com/ansible/latest/installation_guide/intro_installation.html

Inventory:

https://docs.ansible.com/ansible/latest/user_guide/intro_inventory.html

Network Modules:

https://docs.ansible.com/ansible/latest/modules/list_of_network_modules.html

Playbooks:

https://docs.ansible.com/ansible/latest/user_guide/playbooks.html

Developer Guide:

https://docs.ansible.com/ansible/latest/dev_guide/index.html

Ansible and Cisco:

https://www.ansible.com/integrations/networks/cisco

Cisco DevNet

Homepage:

https://developer.cisco.com/

NetDevOps Live:

https://developer.cisco.com/netdevops/live/

Ansible Learning Labs:

https://learninglabs.cisco.com/lab/ansible-02_ansible-intro/step/1

Ansible Video Series:

https://developer.cisco.com/video/net-prog-basics/05-netdevops/ansible_part_1

Slack

Homepage:

https://slack.com/

Network to Code

Homepage:

http://www.networktocode.com/

GitHub:

https://github.com/networktocode

Ansible Training:

http://www.networktocode.com/network-automation-with-ansible/

IpSpace.net

Homepage:

https://www.ipspace.net/Main_Page

Subscriptions:

https://www.ipspace.net/Subscription

Ansible Training:

https://www.ipspace.net/Building_Network_Automation_Solutions

Network Automation Blogs

Jason Edleman - Author:

http://jedelman.com/

IpSpace.net - Blog:

https://blog.ipspace.net/

Ansible Official Blog:

https://www.ansible.com/blog

Network Lore:

https://networklore.com/blog/

Avatao – How to automate your infrastructure with Ansible in a secure way?

https://blog.avatao.com/How-to-automate-your-infrastructure-with/

Will Robinson – Understanding Ansible Output Structure

http://www.oznetnerd.com/understanding-ansible-output-structure/

Microsoft TFS

Homepage:

https://visualstudio.microsoft.com/tfs/

Microsoft VS Code

Homepage:

https://code.visualstudio.com

Visual Studio Developer Community:

https://developercommunity.visualstudio.com

Printed in Great Britain
by Amazon